William Alsop

Alsop & Störmer Architects

LE GRAND BLEU

MARSEILLES

William Alsop

Alsop & Störmer Architects

ACADEMY

Michael Spens

Hôtel du Département des Bouches-du-Rhône

LE GRAND BLEU

MARSEILLES

We would like to thank the *Conseil Général des Bouches-du-Rhône* for their cooperation during the research of this book.

First published in Great Britain in 1994 by
Academy Editions,
an imprint of Academy Group Ltd
42 Leinster Gardens London W2 3AN
member of VCH Publishing Group

Design
Borja Goyarrola Ispizua

Translation
Francis Graves

Diagrams
Anne Schmilinsky

Photography
Roderick Coyne
Paul Raftery
Joelle Manchion
Graham Wood
Stephen Pimbley
John Linden
Aerial images:
Cerf Blanc
Final model images:
Andrew Putler

Distributed to the trade in the United States of America by St Martin's Press 175 Fifth Avenue New York NY 10010

ISBN 185490 357 8

Printed and bound in Italy

TO MY FATHER   FRANK ALSOP
        1886 ~ 1964

AND MY FATHERLY FRIEND
JOHN KENT
        1929 — 1993

Contents

Blue Exterior, White Interior

THE INHABITANTS ARE THE ESSENCE of a town. Through the centuries Marseilles has built up its image: inseparable from the Mediterranean. Along its edge various peoples have grouped themselves into a unified community. All have, however, left their mark on its urban landscape. Marseilles is oriental, Latin, African and European.

William Alsop, an artist, hence an architect in the primary sense of the word, was able to grasp this taste of life, of quiet certitude that constitutes the soul of multisecular towns built on the coast of *Mare Nostrum*; these towns that generated the culture and history of Europe.

As the architect 'speaks' for the future, the politician that I am is happy to have had as a partner, this imaginative British man inspired by the unique qualities of this town that is my own. Marseilles, at the gateway of the world.

Lucien Weygand
Président du Conseil Général des Bouches-du-Rhône

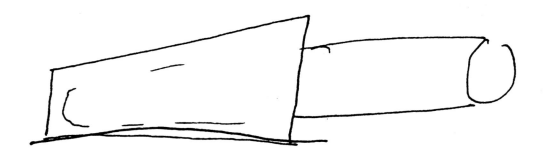

Foreword

THE HOTEL DU DÉPARTEMENT DES Bouches-du-Rhône rapidly became known in its home town, Marseilles, as *Le Grand Bleu*. But Marseilles is a city of diverse opinions, and this title had to win out against a minor faction, who called it for a while '*Maison des Stroumphs*' ('House of the Smurfs'). Either way, affection seems to have blossomed out there. And why Blue? Alsop reminded me when asked, about Yves Klein's preference for the same ultramarine shade of blue. Klein [1] had written:

> *The blue, the gold, the pink, the immaterial, the void, the architecture of the air, the urban planning of the air, the air-conditioning of the great geographic spaces for a return to a human life in nature, in the paradisiac state of legend.*

Le Grand Bleu, Marseilles – referred throughout the book as LE GRAND BLEU – stands for all such dreams, physically embodied in a notable construction that celebrates nothing less than the future of democracy in the twenty-first century. This is not some constructivist vision, such as the Russian architect Chernikhov would have dangled before Soviet citizenry while the egalitarian dreams of Communism descended into an authoritarian abyss. Here, in the ancient capital of the region of France now digitalised as '*Treize*', the Republic's version of regional democracy has materialised through the architecture of William Alsop with appropriate conviction. This political sense is explicit, not least in the architect's own statement here (p. 76). If the institutions of a greater Europe are to work, they must be underpinned by genuine regional democracy.

President Lucien Weygand has been commited to the project since *1990*, ensuring that Alsop was continually encouraged throughout the long gestation and construction of the building.

It is also, therefore, something of a celebration all round that in March *1994*, notwithstanding the high profile kept by the building, the electorate duly re-elected Mr. Weygand as president of the *Conseil Général des Bouches-du-Rhône* for a further term.

So this is no ordinary story; agreed by the architect and author alike that a typical 'freeze-dried' building monograph had to be avoided, despite numerous offers of the genre. Fortunately, Academy Group, under its publisher John Stoddart, was open to ideas and offered continual encouragement. The result is a book published simultaneously in three European languages (thanks also to Academy's sister company within the VCH Group, Ernst & Sohn in Berlin; to Karl Ernst Schneider and Helmut Geisert for their immediate support).

In this narrative form, the saga of the competition came to life, as well as the whole complex process of design development, and on-site construction. Within the Alsop practice, directors Francis Graves and Stephen Pimbley gave valuable contributions, and in Chapter VI describe in their own words the full contract and construction process. Likewise, Jonathan Adams recorded for me the complete account of the competition process, in stages: Chapter III consists largely of his recollections as related from personal experience. Anne Schmilinsky has provided the clearest of diagrams.

To Sybil Diot-Lamige must go unstinted praise for her French translation, and to Marie Neumüllers for the German equivalent. Roderick Coyne, photographer, quietly and incessantly (it seemed) provided a *photo-vérité* of the building process in entirety. Borja Goyarrola who designed the whole book with skill and serendipity, was the crucible without which none of this would have come together so smoothly, if at all.

The tale of how this book actually came out is also one to tell some day, best recounted in the New York bar on the Marseilles waterfront, or the Cooper's Arms, Flood Street, Chelsea (close to the old Alsop office). But the scene moves on.

In Marseilles, special gratitude is due to Alain Bartoli, *Directeur des Services*, Béatrix Billes, *Conseiller technique*,

Patrick Verlinden, *Directeur de la Communication du Conseil Général*, and to Valérie Toche, *attachée de presse*, for encouragement and support.

Finally, Iona Spens, my daughter, is due grateful recognition for her constructive comments concerning the combined texts.

And LE GRAND BLEU, then? Does it even reflect the remarkable teamwork, a kind of *esprit de corps*, which is its testimony? Now it rises over the site (as did those Phocaean Greek colonial temples[2]), representing a human ideal of timeless dimension. Half a century from now we can be more certain of its critical validity – a long time for the media, but a short span for architecture? For the moment, certain correlations with architectures of the recent and more remote past can be made; and such remarkable innovations as the 'X' columns stand out as formidable by any standards. Yet they successfully engage human perceptions about building that run back for centuries. And the computer realisations of building programmes now offer their own poetics.

In the meantime, as this is written, the construction force has all but been disbanded, or been relocated. To these individuals, in the end is surely due the final accolade. As author, I dedicate my own part to those many nameless individuals, adequate testimony I hope to their combined skill and labour.

Michael Spens
Marseilles, July *1994*

1 Yves Klein, *The Votive Offering to Saint Rita de Cascia*
   9 February *1961* (Trans. Pierre Restany)
2 Marseilles was founded by Phocaean Greeks, also responsible for the
   creation of the early temples at Paestum near Naples.

SINGLE FLOOR

Resonances

Marseilles

MARSEILLES HAS A GREAT ADVANTAGE: it has received much
adverse criticism which indicates that it is a town with character.
It is true that Marseilles has no monuments that can compare
with those of its neighbours, Barcelona and Genoa, but in its
favour is its survival against the onslaught of the twentieth
century. The few intrusive exceptions, such as the *quartier de la
Bourse* and the *porte d'Aix* have fortunately been very confined.
It is moreover the pretentious nature of these projects that has
rendered them somewhat difficult to digest; unlike the slab
blocks and towers which have here (in Marseilles) a South-
American feel.

The *unité d'habitation* of Le Corbusier remains, though it
stands very much alone. Le Corbusier was certainly more an
agitator than the founder of a new school of thought. Reality
ran against him. He fought a losing battle. The *unité
d'habitation* is a successful radical achievement, but not
necessarily a model for social housing and urban planning.

In any case, it is evident that what really matters in
Marseilles is the Mediterranean, the sky, the sun and of course
the setting of incredible force, and of wild tortured landscapes of
unbelievable whiteness.

Architecture is not necessarily where one expects to find it.
Le Corbusier asked us to look at the beauty of ocean liners,
aeroplanes and silos. In fact there are silos in Marseilles: silos
and magnificent warehouses. Even better, an elevated motorway
hovers between them. Is this Marseilles' architectural
masterpiece, this motorway which takes you across the docks in
Cinemascope and in Technicolor? What other town in France is
capable of providing such a twentieth century experience? This
motorway possesses complete *Marseillaise* perfection; that is to

say, without fuss. The path taken is exactly where it is required, and if there is an element of magic to this entry into the city it is because it is as simple and direct as a pencil stroke on a plan. It is impossible not to envy those lucky people ascending daily into the sky, who, banking round a panoramic corner, penetrate the heart of the city.

That Marseilles beats all records for the number of elevated roadways (let us call them 'toboggan runs', this is closer to reality) expresses acutely the importance attached to free traffic flow, but perhaps even more so (or so I would like to imagine) a concern for providing the motorist with enlivening experiences.

And why has a refinery never found its way into an architectural book? What do they require to change this? A Marcel Duchamp? To the west of Marseilles there is Berre, Fos, Lavera. At Lavera, the tankers berth as if in a car park. The roads here are lined with protective embankments, behind which are hidden a succession of sparkling oil storage tanks. The refineries intertwined their boilers and their pipe networks, as in hell's basement.

It is extraordinary! The complexity, the know-how and the beauty; it is enough to take one's breath away, especially under the setting sun.

To the east, following the sea, the road stops at Les Goudes. Here deep into a *calanque** are some *cabanons*** self-built from salvaged materials by hands of varying competence, without the intervention of architects, of course. Yet they are full of invention and charm. They are of appropriate scale, and in perfect harmony with the setting.

The *cabanons* are not of minor art, even if they speak more of necessity and liberty than of power. They resemble nothing, are almost spontaneous, they seem naive, yet they prove to be choice ground for the most inspired inventions. These *cabanons*

  * *Rocky inlets to the south of Marseilles*
** *Small simple summer dwellings*

manipulate all forms (without preconceptions but not without sensitivity), all materials especially the most unforgiving, all colours and always with total freedom.

Of course, Marseilles is not only made up of *cabanons*, toboggan runs, isolated cranes and *Cités Radieuses*, the town also has its quarters, its streets, its squares, but it is dissected and fragmented by these structures without architecture and the ever present landscape.

It is the juxtaposition that is exceptional: the superimposition of layers interacting with one another determines and renders this town one of the most successful examples of town planning and urban design of the late twentieth century. To create a metropolis, that is to say to organise the congestion that is of its essence, one must deal with each function in a radical way and superimpose each layer thus created.

Alsop

About Alsop, let us say first of all that he does not lack a sense of humour; a rare trait in architecture, and seems never bored or keen to inflict moral arguments upon one. When, in the early eighties, he started to attract attention, architecture was in a rather desperate state. The front stage was taken up by polemic conflicts between the defenders of an undiluted modernism and the advocates of a sea change that mixed light-weight classicism with populism in an extremely demagogic cocktail. In the face of the rapid expansion of towns, other more appropriate strategies were required: a new generation of architects, adventurous and unafraid to take up the challenge.

Amongst them, William Alsop had an advantage: he was a student under Cedric Price and subsequently worked for him. Cedric Price is a legendary architect who, despite having few built projects, has proved that architecture can escape all aesthetic norms to adhere more closely to the realities of the present, by accepting its ephemeral nature and recognising the value of improvisation.

What Alsop conceived was incredibly joyful and amusing. His project for *Riverside Studios*, the first published in France, recalls through light-hearted manipulations of stereotypes, those interpretations of Bach by Django Reinhart.

In Hamburg, consulted by the town to revitalise the centre, he proposed an incredible catalogue of wonderful devices, subtle interventions, all precise and magical: glazed roofs on slender columns, a network of light walkways striding across the traffic and kiosks on stilts crowned with transparent canopies as fragile as dragonfly wings.

All the projects that followed confirmed his ability to transform, as if by metamorphosis, life experiences into the image for a town.

The common denominator in his structures is an unexpected imbalance. Revealing is his surprising ability to manipulate forces and forms. They are not read as structural elements but as handwriting, not as a grid but as integral expressive elements. They demonstrate especially an ever-present tendency to disarticulate in order to look for the necessary support elsewhere; a tactic doubtless learned from the docks for it is obviously there, in the superstructures of boats and in the cranes, that one can observe such brilliantly improvised structural assemblies.

Alsop in Marseilles

In Marseilles, Alsop did not have an easy task. His only previous French experience had been his participation in the *European Tower* project at Hérouville-St-Clair where Massimiliano Fuksas had called upon him to help conceive a building that would illustrate a new approach of the town. He drew a sort of golden fish, first floor of a four-man effort completed by the Italian Massimiliano Fuksas, the German Otto Steidle and the Frenchman Jean Nouvel. The completed work constituted a real manifesto promoting complexity, multiplicity and diversity.

The secret of Alsop's success in Marseilles is linked to the fact that he knew how to respond not only to the obvious ambitions of the politicians to endow the department with an exemplary building but also to their hidden desire that this should express the dynamism that provides the key of their decision-making.

He understood that it was not only a question of glorifying the power of their institution but also of providing a veritable command post.

The Alsop project has another quality: its great internal transparency. It is not insignificant that in effect the heart of the building is a void, an immense atrium clear and open to the town, accessible to all; hence confirming that the *Hôtel du Département* is not an inaccessible citadel.

It is also a catalyst. Certainly an object, but not isolated because it interacts with the town, responding to a specific location and livening up an uneventful quarter. Like the coastal motorway, like the cranes in the docks, like the *cabanons*, like the *Cités Radieuses* it is without pretence; it does not turn its back on the urban freeways that surround it, it takes up their curves without being subservient to them, affirming its presence, its efficiency and its radical nature.

Like them it puts out of play all recognised aesthetic systems. This is a quality that is common to a certain number of works that have been completed in the last few years and whose forms seem to derive from necessity alone without direct signs of architectural mannerism and whim.

The *Hôtel du Département* is also remarkable by the intelligence with which it thwarts the monolithism and gigantism of such a programme. Thanks to the fragmentation and the subtle balances to which the different volumes respond, the two slab blocks recede into the background in one's perception of the building. The attention has been captured by the unexpected objects of the superstructure and fuselage of the *Deliberatif*, as well as by the various devices that blur, such as the wind deflectors that confuse the edges, the striations of Brian Clarke that establish the façade and, of course, the structural crosses that support the blocks above the ground.

The 'X' columns are particularly ingenious. The problem lies in changing from the parking grid to that of the offices. The usual solution is a transfer beam whose depth can be reduced by struts, as proposed in the first project. The final solution illustrates perfectly Alsop's way of working. It is at once explicit and unexpected. This example shows a reduction process (the crosses operate like a pair of scissors) and an uplifting process (reminiscent of the vehicles that permit the loading and unloading of aeroplane holds).

Another reason to appreciate this building is the importance of the added qualities; for example: the interior square and the terrace below the 'Aerofoil' where astonishment is experienced whilst perceiving this great blue vessel; the sheer pleasure in discovering an interior space as vast and luminous; or again the impression of the reappearance of the sea on a site abandoned until now, communicating a transfer of energy, space and this feeling of power and efficiency all through the appearance of this oasis.

Less is more

Of course, those who have seen and examined in detail the projects of the first and second phases of the competition can but question the transformations that the project experienced. They are proof that the battles must have been tough, and the first reaction is to sympathise with Alsop, imagining that if the building has changed so much, it is because he lost many battles. However, on reflection, it is not quite so evident. Could he have exploited these struggles in order to bring more power and more authenticity to his building? One of the problems of architecture today is surely that it is always close to pleonasm. Each building is conceived to be coherent, its unity clearly defined, the possibility of interaction restrained; an inviolate architecture.

The competition project, even fragmented, had this homogeneous aspect along with a constructional functional perfection and characteristic aesthetic. It was like a fashion model, perfect from head to toe, but at the same time

inaccessible. It was hit hard, very hard, and left with a black eye, a broken nose and cauliflower ears, but it gained from this an authenticity and an indisputable charm; just like Humphrey Bogart! It became more accessible, more open, more human.

For example: the offices. It is true that the first solution provided the grouping of offices with more fluid communication, that the circulation on gangways would have transformed the atriums into permanently animated spaces. It is true, too, that the final solution is fairly classic and corresponds, surely, closer to the requirements of the users and to the financial constraints. This does not prevent the metamorphosis of the use of these standard office spaces through the view and the astonishing route one must take to reach them.

The comparison between the transverse sections is significant. Those of the first project are magnificent; those of the built scheme rather brutal. One could easily believe that they were drawn without an architect as workshop technical drawings of a factory component. In reality they translate into one of the most impressive spaces of the *Hôtel du Département*: this rift dividing the stark cliffs of offices whose summit is animated by the appearance of the rounded flanks of the 'Aerofoil' and the fuselage of the *Deliberatif*, is of an architectural sensuality unsurpassed to this day.

In Marseilles, William Alsop has thus succeeded in grasping the essence of the setting and the spirit of the age.

Patrice Goulet

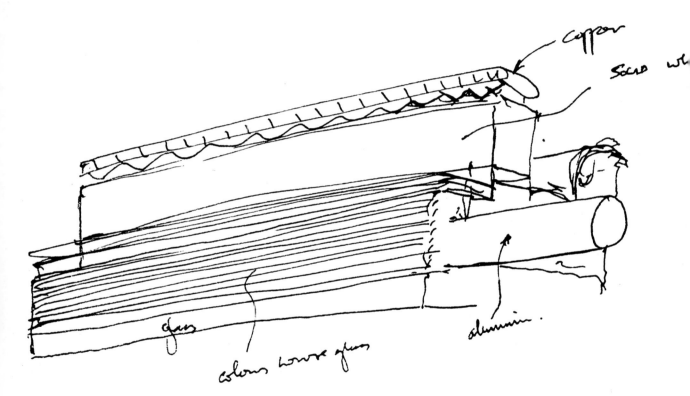

Copper

Solid we

glass

colours louvre glass

alumini.

The Story as Built

THE STORY OF LE GRAND BLEU IS not really about an object, but about human beings in space creating a process; activity that ends with a building, the subject of all their endeavours.

The building is the imprint of all those endeavours from the time when the competition was won, in July *1990* until *1994* (a very short time in the history of Marseilles, but significant); from the initial idea in the mind of the architect, to the first cigarette smoked by an occupant on the terrace; from that split second in the mind of an architect, to another split moment of relaxation in one spot: perhaps for the smoker it is sunset and the draw on the cigarette glows the moment that the sun tilts silently below the Mediterranean horizon. This story happens to fill a book, but really only a movie would capture all the activity of all the people who together came to make LE GRAND BLEU, the building.

And it just happens that the architect was surprised to find as it rose up several storeys, that the building really did look like the scale models built initially to convey its form. Not many buildings do. But, as the Marseillais always knew, LE GRAND BLEU is different, which is the only reason why it is worth making the book tell the story. This presence came to fill the lives of a construction force composed of numerous individuals. Once they built it; now it lives on in their memories. Documents have their uses.

To the citizens of Marseilles, LE GRAND BLEU is still a subject of fervent discussion, and mostly of pride. Two years ago a fibreglass boat, a replica of a fifteenth century galleon built by Roman Polanski, stayed for a while in the harbour of Marseilles. It was later sent away for renovation and is now back. This vessel is different however: to many, it represents the new Marseilles, or more correctly, the spirit of a new Marseilles, since it is unforgettable once you have experienced it. There is also the

View from the 'Aerofoil' balcony, level 9, looking south.

Photo of final model, taken from the north end.

special satisfaction that such a building could never get built in Paris today. As you look down from the *Deliberatif*, on the downward dual carriageway gradient, such has been the erosion to the macadam caused by the braking every day of thousands of Provence commuters who glimpse momentarily LE GRAND BLEU, that you can see signs of repeated re-surfacing. There they go again. It's that kind of event.

And the architect? Nowadays architects are not well understood; in England, less than ever before. The profession is being downgraded in priority, as if professional vocation was a restrictive practice, no less, and loses respect because by the code of the *1980*'s it did not respect money alone as the principal and only value criterion. The architect? He was William Alsop, supporter of traditional professional modes; interpreting these in a precise manner that reminds one of the *chef d'atelier* of the nineteenth century. The architect above all continues still as artist, creator, and one who develops architectural ideas as if they were poetry.

The first idea of LE GRAND BLEU was undoubtedly a line drawing, produced freely in the notebook; but the second was a painting. Colour and form freely associated as conveyors of the idea, from the start. Numerous line drawings thus emerged from the notebook, and paintings dripped swiftly onto canvas. These were the first firm expressions of a fleeting idea that was nevertheless entirely technical, and eminently buildable. Really, it is not meant to happen that way any more. But it does, in the best hands.

What then did these drawings and paintings constitute? Firstly a reconnaissance into territory not entirely unexplored.

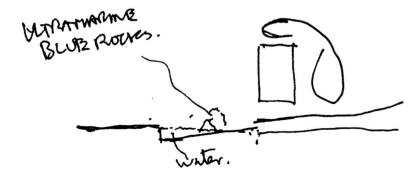

Model for *Expo '92* project.

Previous page: View of the Atrium under construction with 'Ovoid'.

This space has traces of the (*1989–1990*) Seville *Expo '92* design for which Alsop was premiated. For some time the balloon that so distinguished the Seville entry lingered also over the three original blocks for Marseilles, vying with the cigar shaped *Deliberatif* for the attention of the client. One day it was gone, spawning yet another model in the process.

The architect all this time kept his nerve and stayed within the exacting contingency margins imposed by the quantity surveyors. To be fair, they had little of substance built by Alsop to go on as yet. The best way to understand LE GRAND BLEU, is to realise it, is to consider it not so much as an object, but as a 'subjective' phenomenon. Thus it represents ideas evolved through drawing, contemplation, speculation, and rationalisation. LE GRAND BLEU is different from most buildings in that it is a work that literally embodies process; it is a schema, a formula, which develops its own dynamic. The guiding codes of this momentum are only such as are predicated by buildability and constructional feasibility – implying degrees of greater or lesser automatisation and industrialised building techniques – as well as by its usability, and its degree of functional coherence and 'fit'.

Throughout the process, there has been a positive disarticulation; a testing process whereby the architect has retained the option to make amendments. These 'variables' are

Watercolour sketch.

clearly not of the main structure, but can apply within secondary and tertiary levels of assembly, as adaptations on site.

A particular case in point is that of the *Deliberatif* the section which, clearly separated and linked by access bridges to the *Administratif* blocks, contains those places where the elected representatives of les Bouches-du-Rhône make their governmental decisions. The cladding, of triangular-shaped panels, set on a double curvature, is constructed so as to allow rainwater to run-off underneath these 'scales', with the definitive solution being developed with the contractor on site.

Alsop on site.

Here the architect functions in the process not only as composer, but as conductor; the score of course can be amended in the process of playing. The fine point here is that the architecture is not all freeze-dried while work proceeds. This building is also a statement about the role of the profession. In fact there is nothing new in history about the master–builder, whether under the Pharaohs or in the Gothic cathedral-building period. But latterly, something vital has been lost en route. Human fallibility, apathy, and a lack of intellectual rigour have conspired through the increasing sophistication of building management systems, to drop the architect as conductor, preferably as soon as site operations commence. The Marseilles process ensured the continued presence of William Alsop and has demonstrated the importance of the architect as the professional who exercises and fulfils the greatest degree of professional responsibility possible.

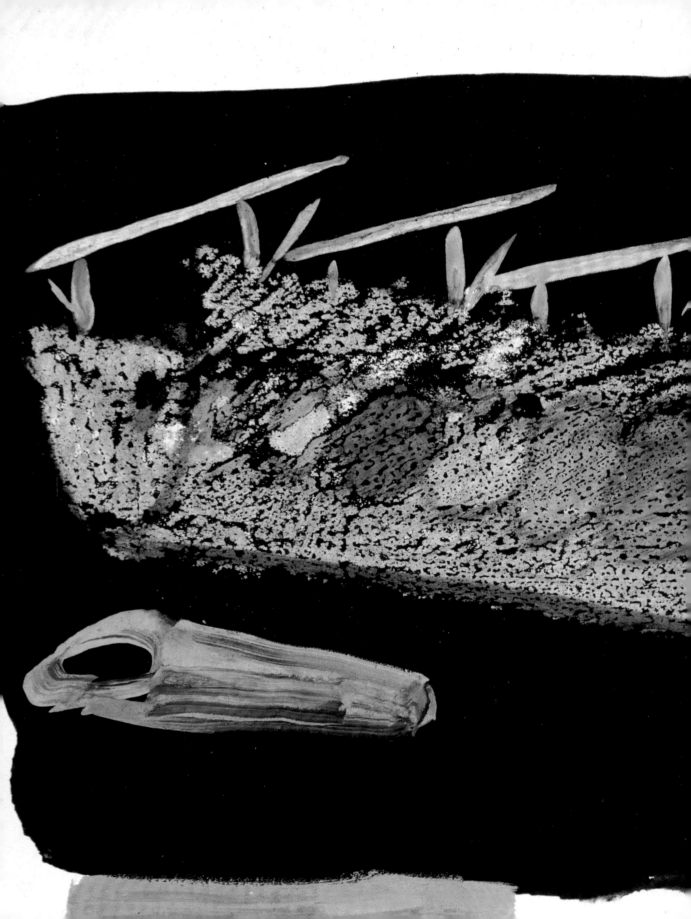

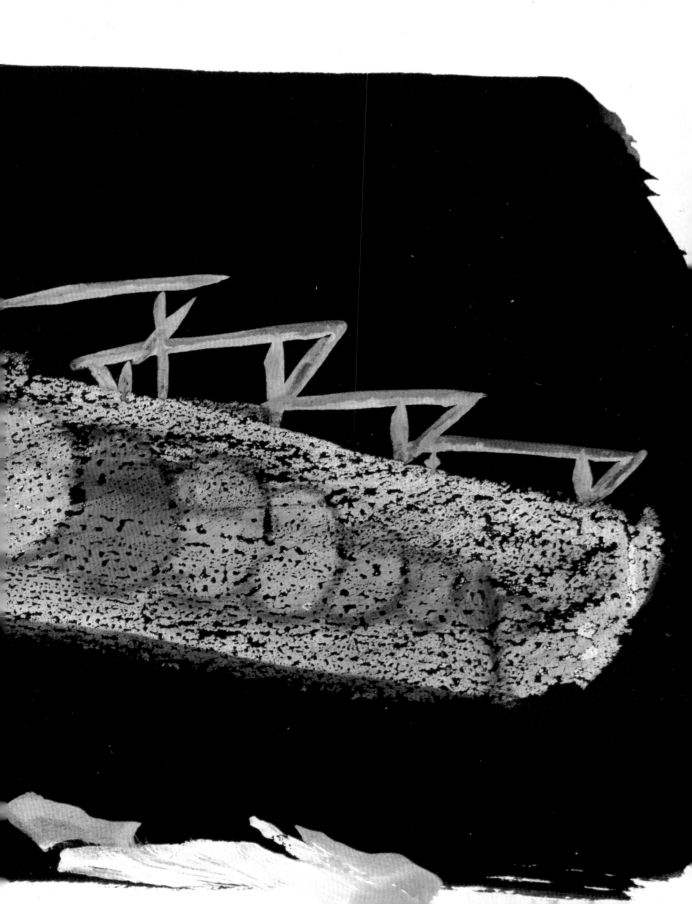

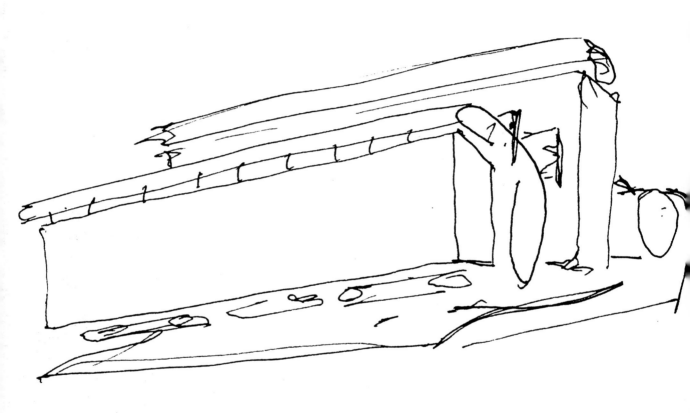

How It Happened

LE GRAND BLEU HAPPENED AS the result of an open competition. A now legendary gladiatorial contest established the winner in a final round with Sir Norman Foster and William Alsop, in which the outcome seemed predictable wherein the former would be proclaimed victor and the latter, the promising young outsider would lose graciously to generous applause.

Overall view of building during construction taken from the south.

There had been *156* entrants in the first round, amongst them some of the most talented international architects with a strong and predominant French entry; including, respectively, Gino Valle and Pascal Urban in the final line-up.

The department of les Bouches-du-Rhône was determined to achieve an outstanding and original building for its new headquarters and seat of government, on a site located carefully in a less than prosperous quarter on the outskirts of the city of Marseilles, set in a prominent position adjoining an important road intersection approaching the inner city.

The announcement that William Alsop had been selected as the winner came as a thunderbolt within the architectural world. International competitions are a means whereby, especially in open contest, younger architects at least have the chance to show their talent on the international stage; seldom does new talent actually win, although it is often compensated with second or third prize awards, or otherwise commended. Such had already been Alsop's experience long ago in the *1971 Centre Pompidou* competition for Beaubourg, Paris.

In retrospect, the jury had behaved commendably in Marseilles. It had pursued great diligence in running a final round between the two architects preferred from those selected in the penultimate contest. It had wanted to be absolutely certain that it would get the best and had displayed a complete internationalism in accepting the pre-eminence of two foreign architects, Foster and Alsop, to run against each other to the ultimate exclusion of the French competitors.

In fact a critical regionalism had won out against the tradition of Cartesian rationale which still commands a powerful allegiance in France, and especially in Paris. Beyond France too, this result has to be recognised historically as the decisive setback for the 'post-modernist' ascendancy which had in the *1980*'s so effectively capitalised upon the politically fashionable rejection of modernism in Western cultural centres; temporary and short-lived as that can now recognisably be seen to have been. For here was a scheme that utilised contemporary technology and yet embraced the particularities of regional climate and environmental conditions. In this proposal the roots of modernism could be clearly recognised, and yet there was a looseness and flexibility, an openness that fed through from philosophy to design details. Here was a project different from the air-conditioned envelope proffered by its competitors. In Marseilles, it seemed that journalists and commentators were acutely aware of the problems raised by the recent Paris-based competition for the *Bibliothèque Nationale* (National Library) where the seemingly simplistic glass 'book-ends' of Dominique Perrault had won. Yet in Marseilles a hermetically sealed and glazed counterpart by Foster was poised seemingly to win out.

Roof terrace and wind deflector of block A under construction.

But it was not to be. Following a rigorous testing process well beyond expectations, it was found that the Alsop scheme offered distinct advantages in operational and environmental terms; and perhaps too, where 'conscience', social and ecological, was concerned. Not that monumentality was a quality to be overlooked either. The daily journal *Le Provençal*, in particular, praised the Alsop entry as *'un monument de convivialité'*. Here lies the real clue to 'why Alsop', the question on the lips of the cognoscenti gathered in London to celebrate the anticipated Foster victory.

There is an attitude to enjoyment and the quality of life that is well-balanced and is the product of centuries of social development in this part of France. The minimalist ethos has affinities in the French mind with Calvinism, a non-conformism historically banished here to the mountains. Alsop, in life as in work, expresses that tradition of conviviality.

Memories of Le Corbusier, another refugee in exile from such persuasions, run long in this part of France, where he died swimming out from his *'petit cabanon'* under the azure sky. In the *unité d'habitation*, Le Corbusier had sought over a quarter of a century earlier to create a paradigm of local conditions. In older parts of Marseilles high and narrow streets protect the inhabitants from the direct rays of the sun, providing shelter from the mistral wind as it sweeps overhead for weeks on end at varying times of the year. The warmed air is drawn upwards, drying washing rapidly before escaping into the blue sky. Streets lie shuttered around midday, for protection; in the evening, windows and shutters are thrown open for conviviality; in the early morning likewise, for cooling. Here, Le Corbusier found himself evoking the Hellenic past, where Marseilles had been founded originally by Phocaean Greeks in the sixth century BC, passing northwards from the sacred outpost of Paestum, resplendent with great temples.

Arguably, those CIAM members assembled in *1954* on the sculptured roof terrace of the *unité d'habitation* could have dreamed up a further invocation of this heritage (as

Model photograph of preliminary design for entrance stairs and ramps.

Detail of *Deliberatif* and bridge connecting to block B.

contemplated perhaps from the promenade deck of the SS Patras): the vision materialises as Alsop's very own crystal-blue model floating boldly past.

At the *unité d'habitation*, Le Corbusier had transformed two previous tenets of this architecture. The wall, as surface, had now become polyvalent (from gridded void to solid mass, to polychromatic mosaic); and the *brise-soleil* came to be applied here as never before. Le Corbusier relied for air change on a natural symbiosis brought about by the interaction of air currents. The creation of the *unité d'habitation* allowed him to draw these inhabitants right back to context. At the same time he led them in a celebration of their Greek antecedents, recalling a classical humanism deeply rooted in the Mediterranean. The *unité d'habitation* roof terrace enshrines the Homeric foredeck of legend, but at the same time the sculptured elements that enhance the long terrace endorse communal activities such as jogging as well as nursery activities. The spirit is nothing if not convivial.

LE GRAND BLEU acknowledges such tradition and precedent without reservation. Alsop has however reached his own accommodation between past and future along a different and protracted route, itself based upon new experimentation. Repeated technical and aesthetic sorties have developed a design mode wholly of the late twentieth century yet of undoubted originality. There is an inevitable and determined distancing from the masters. Any permissible referencing can only apply to specific attitudes about the actual making of architecture expressed through the permanently present notebook, through painting (as a further kind of note-making), and by means of a more or less continuous dialectical exchange, pursued both within the office and with close friends and artists, such as Mel Gooding and Bruce McLean.

This process is also responsive to location at a given time. In Australia, for example, a remote testing ground often re-visited by Alsop, he recorded the lesson of the eucalyptus tree, whose leaves must change direction so that they always present their

Right: View from roof terrace of block A looking north.

West façade.

edge condition to the fierce sun. The collective hedonism of the ocean beach is imported within the *Sheringham Leisure Pool* (Norfolk, England *1985*), with displayed flush-fitting impregnated timber panels for external cladding that are strongly reminiscent of the work of Jean Prouvé. The idiom of Prouvé was present in early work on Marseilles, but not in specific detailing: this is not Alsop's way.

From early projects when Alsop attended (and later taught at) Saint Martin's School of Art, off Covent Garden, London, and through a more or less compatible working relationship with Cedric Price (a key player in the post-Brutalist reorientation of British architectural thinking in the *1970*'s), an early awareness of ecological and environmental factors in design manifested itself. At the time when initial ideas for Marseilles were in gestation, Alsop had just completed highly imaginative proposals for the river Garonne at Bordeaux (*1989*). This programme of enhancement compensated for the withdrawal and gradual disappearance of the once constant stream of great coloured vessels from the tidal reaches of the river Garonne; new colours emerged to float (by means of numerous devices, such as propaganda sails, inflated balloons, and electrically opening flowers). Alsop's concept here for a *Cathédrale Engloutie* as a Garonne activator involved not a bridge (this item was given to another competitor to grapple with) but a long, submerged structure, following the directional flow line of the natural river current. This was to be a kind of elemental 'belvedere', from which the public could both observe and feel the clouds in the Atlantic sky, the flows of the river, and the historic views up and down the Garonne.

The most immediate and dramatic precursor to LE GRAND BLEU, however, was undoubtedly the project for *EXPO '92*, Seville. This drew upon specific local climatic factors. Traditional ways of installing natural cooling by means of water conduits and pools (designed to assist evaporation cooling) were developed. An opening roof was incorporated to stimulate vertical airflows and ambient cross-currents. A reliable temperature control system was thus available to mediate the display space micro-climatically; all was integrated within the ultimate building form. This scheme won second place. Nicholas Grimshaw & Partners were commissioned.

The experience derived from the *1989–1990 Hamburg Ferry Terminal* building was undoubtedly instrumental in the track of acquired proficiency for the practice, both in London and Hamburg. However there are certain clear precedents in this scheme that had a bearing upon the design solution for Marseilles, especially in the mode of transfer structure marking the differing planning grid of the offices above and the terminal floor below.

The arrival of the Marseilles commission in the Alsop office has enabled ideas which were conceived for a disparate range of projects, touched upon briefly here, to merge effectively. The designs for Bordeaux, Seville and Hamburg in particular possessed qualities of identity, ecology, structural rationale, and climatic optimisation, all of which are expressly apparent in LE GRAND BLEU. Above all, an absolute responsiveness to the real rather than conventionally assumed needs of the ultimate occupants of the building was, in Alsop's book, considered to be of paramount importance.

Roof terrace of *unité d'habitation* looking towards the gymnasium.

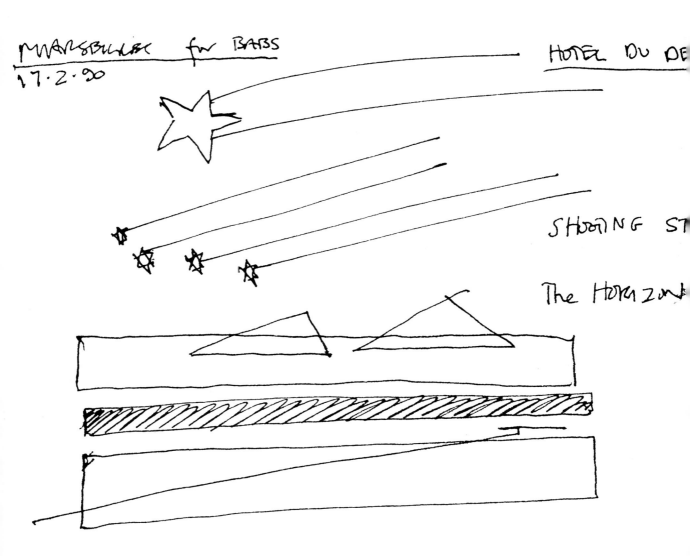

MARSBULGE for BABS

17.2.90

HOTEL DU DE

SHOOTING ST

The Horizon

The Competition Saga

ĞVT.

THE NARRATIVE THAT constitutes LE GRAND BLEU cannot be left
freeze-dried. The building now lives, and will continue to exist
only insofar as it meets human aspiration for daily shelter,
assembly, convenience and also identity. Today the whole
community of Marseilles.and the surrounding area of les
Bouches-du-Rhône, now associate with this building the
concerns of future government. They, the electorate, claim it as
their achievement, 'anchored' on the edge of their capital city; a
strong blue form, so sculptured and multi-faceted that it is easy
to orientate by its respective profiles, by day or by night.

Competition programme.

It is significant that the building first came about through an
open architectural competition: that most random and accident-
prone method of selection. It says much for the determination of
President Weygand, the president of the council of the
departmental government, that no short cuts were taken, and no
stalling or deviation occurred in favour of one faction or another
– a hazard for which such contests are notorious.

In the Alsop office in London, now located on the south end
of the elegant Albert Bridge over the Thames, much has
changed. New architectural competitions follow one another in
rapid sequence. Fortunately one individual, Jonathan Adams,
made a written record of the whole process of the Marseilles
competition, as one of the small nucleus of architects that were
involved with Alsop. This has proved to be an invaluable record
in establishing the actual facts here.

As Adams describes in his own record of events concerning
the competition, the practice at this time constituted some ten
individuals who had worked on some two hundred and fifty
different schemes by *1990*, only a handful of which had been
built. The actual invitation from Marseilles, to participate in the
competition came out of the blue:

It was written in a foreign language – it almost got filed in the bin. Will was in Australia [...] but because of that letter within a few surreal months there were over a hundred of us.

The letter was thus not granted undue significance. But the result was to transform the future of the firm. Alsop's first two conceptual sketches were the result of only a few days consideration of the brief. A group of three raised blocks together with an adjacent tubular structure within a kind of rib cage, all elevated above a 'scooping ground plan' allowed the intervening spaces to be 'capped with tubular airships', as the office described them.

It is important to remember that this was not long after Alsop had gained second place in the Seville *Expo' 92* British Pavilion competition. While this had been a chastening experience, the attitude that now prevailed at Alsop's was both

Diagrammatic cross-section.

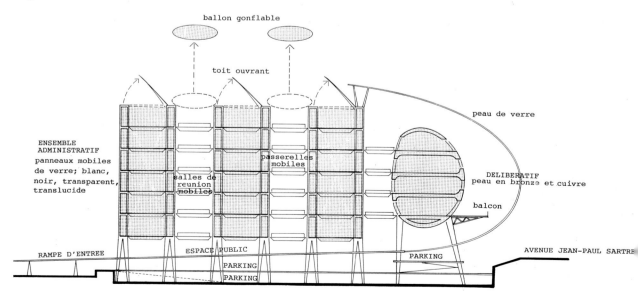

speculative and at the same time cooler and more measured, forged on the anvil so to say.

Stage I Competition

The requisite two panels as submitted by the Alsop practice were laid out as collaged plans, accompanied by a key cross-section. Photographs of the first model reiterated what were essentially realisations of the cross-sections and oblique views that had emerged earlier from the pages of the Alsop notebook. There was also (on the panels) a minimal engineering input showing in diagrammatic form the environmental principles involved. Evidently, seen against the mass of 155 other entries, these brightly coloured photo-montages were able to draw the jury's attention most effectively.

Panels for Stage I.

The Deliberatif

From this outset, the clear separation of parts in the scheme was self-evident, allowing the debating chamber, the *Deliberatif*, to stand out:

> *We have located the 'Deliberatif' in a strong form which is designed to be read at speed. To the east is Avenue Jean-Paul Sartre which contains traffic moving at speed […]. Here we have a building that responds to speed and the behaviour of people in this part of the city.*
> William Alsop

It is clear that while Alsop's interest, at Stage 1, was concentrated on the massing of the whole and of the surface treatment of the glass double-walls, he was most concerned with the internal and external qualities of the *Deliberatif*. Alsop insisted that the Council Chamber should be a memorable and important place.

Just as these priorities and semblances were sustained throughout the whole competition process, elements of a design idiom originating with Alsop's old mentor, Cedric Price, also survived throughout: the supports to the intermediate floors, the bridges between the administrative blocks and also between the eastern block and the *Deliberatif*, were retained determinedly, together with a 'rack-like idiom' as Adams refers to it – clearly integral to the office's way of thinking.

The emergence of the *Deliberatif*, in 'chrysalis' form at this first stage, having already established its own mystique as a centre of power, was not accidental.

The building will witness in its own history important decisions that will impact on the lives of many people who live and work in the region. For this reason we have designed a building that will in its organisation reflect a democracy that will prevail in the activities of the politicians and civil servants working in it. The main body of offices is non-hierarchical providing a system of occupation that will offer a flexible distribution of departments. Uncertainty in the future means that nothing should be determined now. Lying outside the system is the 'Deliberatif'. This element of the building is apart in order to reflect the nature of the

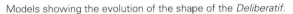

Models showing the evolution of the shape of the *Deliberatif*.

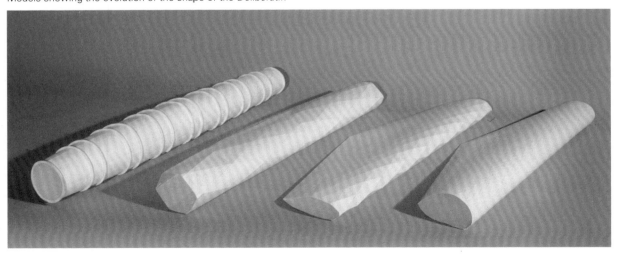

activities that it contains. *The process of political debates should take place within a 'calm' environment. Decisions should not be rushed. The spaces should be generous and the interior of the main chamber should not change. It should remain a vessel of remembrance, a place that acquires a sense of its own history.*
William Alsop

Stage I model.

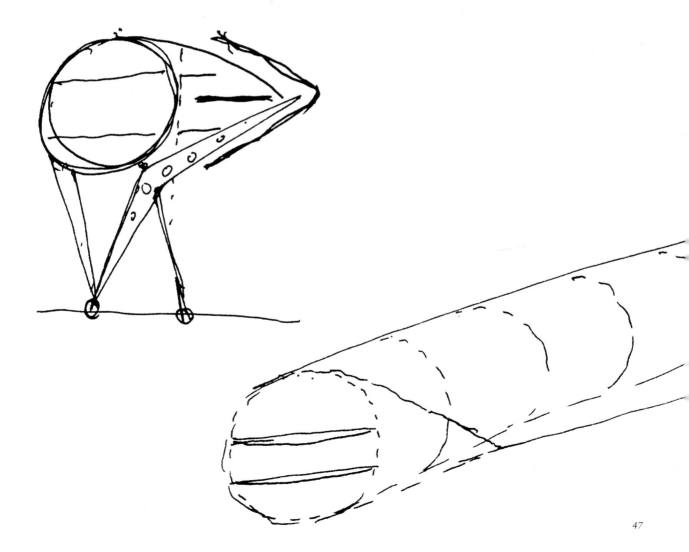

The Administratif Blocks

Most important also, in the key line-up of elements at the first stage of the competition were the double glass walls, considered emblematically, as Adams relates.

> *The imagining of the double glass walls was precise in scope and detail. All the circulation in the 'Administratif' blocks was contained within these. The narrow spaces would have been threaded with walkways [...] You would be moving along between two, apparently endless glass planes, lateral sunlight streaming through, filtered and dappled, fresh air moving freely upwards and along. This is such a compelling experiential mechanism that Will might have felt obliged to commission music, as he is wont to do, to be played within those spaces, to complete the enchantment.*

As the design rationale proceeded, apart from the glass double-walls, which nonetheless had a compelling effect in the initial line-up (in specific contrast with the *Deliberatif*'s mass for example), the opening roofs atop the administratif blocks were dropped. And in this fall-out of Seville memorabilia, the air-ship roofs above the atria, the scooping entrance ramp, and the external 'rib-cage' of the *Deliberatif* all disappeared, in the name of rationalisation.

DEP.
DRH

49

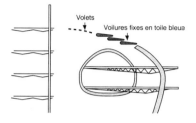

The Engineers

Ove Arup International's members, played a key role initially in the development of the scheme; earlier too, they had been instrumental in the evolution of the Seville entry by the Alsop practice. While not involved in the very earliest concept development by Alsop for Marseilles, their innovative environmental engineering ideas were influential. Alsop realised that the client in Marseilles showed a clear political will to embrace 'green' solutions. In the initial scheme, the glass double wall had acted as buffer zones, while the atria, the opening roofs, and the high bulk of the *Administratif* blocks would channel air upwards throughout the building, warmed or cooled as required. The scheme was validated at a technical level from the beginning.

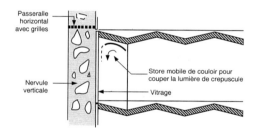

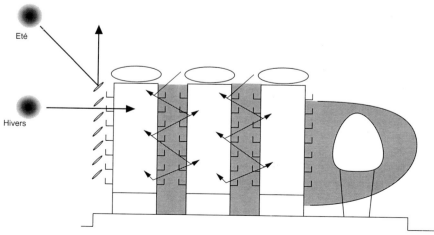

CONTROLE DE LA LUMIERE DU JOUR ET DU SOLEIL

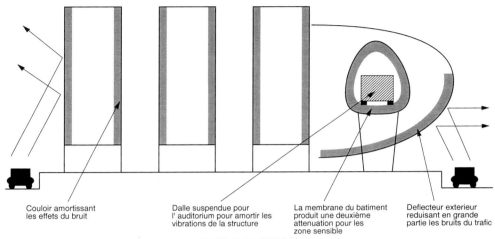

Couloir amortissant
les effets du bruit

Dalle suspendue pour
l' auditorium pour amortir les
vibrations de la structure

La membrane du batiment
produit une deuxième
attenuation pour les
zone sensible

Deflecteur exterieur
reduisant en grande
partie les bruits du trafic

CONTROL ACOUSTIQUE

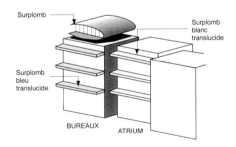

Surplomb

Surplomb
blanc
translucide

Surplomb
bleu
translucide

BUREAUX   ATRIUM

Initial environmental studies developed
by Ove Arup International.

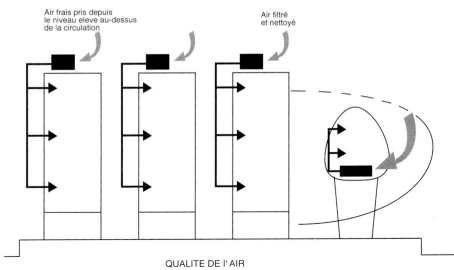

Air frais pris depuis
le niveau eleve au-dessus
de la circulation

Air filtré
et nettoyé

QUALITE DE l' AIR

Stage II Competition

Once the Alsop scheme had been selected therefore for Stage II, Ove Arup & Partners were able to be brought into the official team, since the financial basis now existed to establish a multi-disciplinary team.

Initial Changes

The *Deliberatif* now began to change again; mechanically louvred blades now filled the space between the ribbed structures, while the scaly 'carapace' offered its own solution to the adequate ventilation of the well-populated parliamentary and conference chambers within. It was essential that the skin of the *Deliberatif* should become a breathing system, a permeable membrane. Nothing now remained remotely diagrammatic. The first stage *Deliberatif* had a single balcony, using the in-between space in the two skins; but the second version now offered more generously two wide decks, which thus became a prominent visual characteristic.

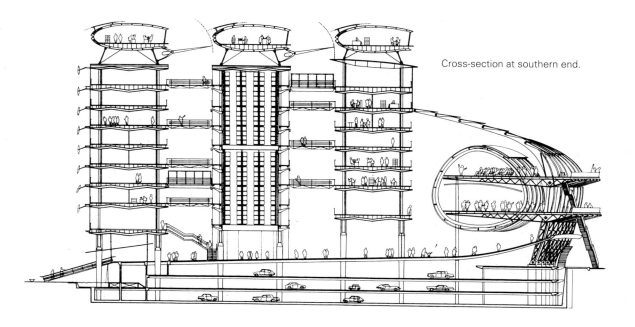

Cross-section at southern end.

Structural System

At this stage the fundamental structural system of the building had not finally been chosen. To Alsop it was becoming rapidly clear that as in the firm's earlier *Hamburg Ferry Terminal* building (*1988*) concrete was the ideal structural material. Ove Arup International were already committed to concrete floor slabs. This also led to the elimination of suspended ceilings, which pleased Alsop. The gull-wing floor slabs were now introduced to great advantage.

At this point in Stage *11* a detailed accommodation brief stipulated a reduction of *15* per cent in accommodation needs. The full effects of the world-wide recession were having an effect in Marseilles. Whereupon the central of the three *Administratif* blocks was dramatically reduced, creating further open space. Here at roof level the top deck of the central block was to remain tied in a flying roof deck complete with sports hall, gymnasium and tennis courts.

Stage II model.

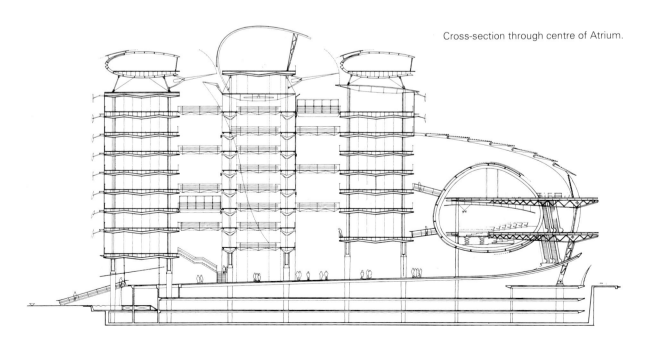

Cross-section through centre of Atrium.

As Adams points out:

This is the only version of the Marseilles scheme through which two distinct cross sections can be drawn: one through the solid three blocked mass of the 'Administratif' with similar sleek aerofoil structures on top of each, and the other through the arch of the sports hall's fabric roof, in the centre. The two sections are quite different, and in terms of the variety of its elements, the second of the two cross-sections is the one that is closer to the finished building.

The central space was now developing into a cavern. Alsop now proposed a remarkable installation: a suspended curtain sweeping down in a 'S' curve from parapet level down to mezzanine. A diaphanous veil of gauze was contemplated. Alsop relished the involvement of acoustic engineers and new possibilities of a hitherto unpredictable installation occurred.

Further Changes

At this crucial stage further new changes were to occur. The removal of the opening flaps at roof level over the atrium led directly to the creation of the 'aerofoils' on top of the *Administratif* blocks. Each 'aerofoil' in prototype form housed a floor of specialised accommodation, such as the library, executive suites, and presidential quarters. The characteristic 'C' format had derived from Alsop's *Hamburg Ferry Terminal* competition scheme. To the nucleus of longer-serving staff in the office it was the welcome re-appearance of an old friend.

An extruded form now took over, creating a visual dynamic that gave the whole, revised version an underlying unity. The two blocks of the remaining *Administratif* seem to hold a potential for infinite extension, in theory at least: but the firm abutment of the *Deliberatif* constrains this dynamic, anchors the whole complex, and re-asserts its more decisive function. The paradox is, in typical Alsop manner, that this is achieved not by the overall articulation of related parts to a static conclusion (a frequent result in early modernist building); instead it is characterised by a visible 'disarticulation' of the separate parts, creating an apparent looseness and flexibility.

By this stage in the competition the temperature was beginning to rise both inside and outside the Alsop offices in the Chelsea Power House. It was no surprise that in the select list of firms invited to proceed to Stage *I I*, Foster Associates was already assumed to be the favourite, and had also possibly considered itself to be the likely winner. Now the Alsop entry became the receptacle for superficial changes, yet such tactical amendments were vital in the line-up for the final selection. The requisite model became white, as if to equate with Foster's sales pitch of invincible technology. Ove Arup International now made its own in-house CAD facilities available to the project team. Such telling images (of an inherent crudity that seemed to iron out and render seamless the ever-present curves of Alsop's design) would impress certain members of the jury. A bonus for the evolution of the design itself occurred as a result – the CAD modelled versions of the transfer structure (as devised originally by Arup's Chris McCarthy) offered figurative supports like 'trunks with outstretched arms', but from these sprang the profile of the 'X' columns that now characterise so particularly the building structure at ground level and resolve the prominent aspect of load transference.

Stage II model.

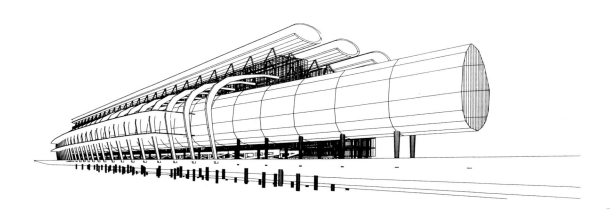

The Final Selection: Stage III

The decision of the competition organisers and jury to opt for a final contest between Alsop and Foster alone, showed that Alsop's intermediate tactic (making 'safe' the scheme, and 'white like Foster') had worked remarkably well. It implied that the two schemes, two of a kind, were so close that it was only thorough and fair to extract both for a final contest. In retrospect, it can seem a wholly Gallic and dramatic variation – in England it could never have happened. It suggests considerable intelligence, and diligence, on the part of the client and jury. The concept of the final gladiatorial duel is deeply implanted in the Mediterranean sensibility, Grecian even in its origins. One wonders whether it was not at this point that a small cloud the size of a man's hand (Le Corbusier type, modular hand upstretched) did not cross the spectrum of the Foster office team. To Alsop it offered the first indication that victory was not impossible. The Alsop team, as Adams' diary

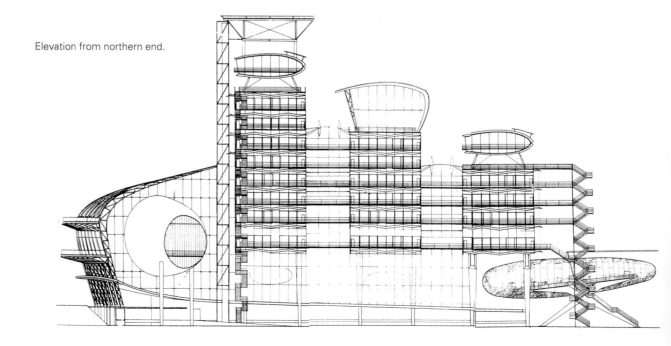

Elevation from northern end.

relates, was: 'exhausted. The sudden invention of the third stage […] was as agonising as it was thrilling.'

The competition accommodation brief was now reduced again. This led Alsop to take up the opportunity given, to substantially redesign the main elements. In Alsop's design method a building must be imagined as a sequential experience, 'disarticulated', yet with specific assemblages that follow upon each other, and become as a rule named 'events' – such as the 'Ovoid', the 'Aerofoil', the 'Cloud' – developing their own formal autonomy. The mass of the *Deliberatif* itself was now lowered too, and the adjacent bloc of the *Administratif* next to it was raised in reflex. This was intended to play down any hasty presumption about the *Deliberatif* in the jury's mind. Nothing was left to chance.

Just as the heat was really being turned on, Alsop was playing a high-risk hand. Such too could unhinge an opponent, or at least his supporters within the jury, opening up fixed lines, turning the game.

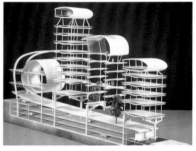

Stage III sectional model.

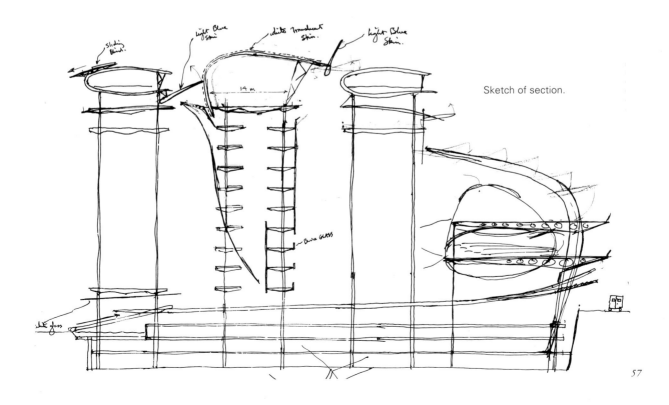

Sketch of section.

Final Challenge

The Stage *III* model now took on a key explanatory role. It was the first to be made at *1:200* scale. The colour, so redolent of Alsop's intentions, muted at Stage *II*, now flowed back in profusion. By now Alsop was producing numerous water-colour sketches and was thinking in 'free colour' increasingly. Just as the Foster team had been lulled into contemplating the approximations of approach between the two opposing schemes on the evidence displayed at Stage *II*, Alsop was now preparing every move to emphasise the absolute contrast between his and theirs. It was a reasonable assumption now that the jury had already been satisfied that the combination of Alsop, Arup and Hanscomb Ltd, the quantity surveyors, was as 'sound' a prospect as that offered by Foster: both teams could build equally well their buildings.

Now also the plaza below began to teem with life. The drawings included a perspective of the open space thronged with figures around a kind of maypole, itself supporting a type of

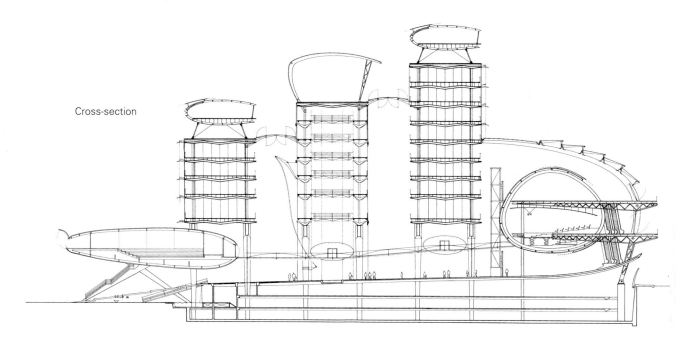

Cross-section

parasol. From the *Cardiff Bay Visitors' Centre* came the prototype for two ovoid free-standing structures which acted as discrete conference houses inside the Atrium.

Stage III full model.

> *The floor of arrival is large. It is conceived as part of the city. The external space must flow into the building. It is here that the café is situated in order to give life to the space. The main reception/information point is also here. It is envisaged that visitors to the building will be asked to wait on the floor of arrival. Here they will find tobacco and newspaper shops as well as coffee opportunities. A liberal scattering of comfortable seats will also be provided. It is our intention to avoid the normal situation in institutional building of a number of small, badly serviced uncomfortable waiting rooms. We aim to lift the spirit.*
>
> *As the visitor uses the floor of arrival he will become aware of the administrative offices above. The bridges between the two buildings through the atrium courtyard will give evidence of life. We wish to avoid the closed building which is why it is also important to have opening windows to the offices. Individual desire for privacy inside boxes is a sign of conceit and lethargy. As one enters the building from the west it is possible to see right through to the skyline. This building should not represent a barrier. This building will glow at night.*

William Alsop

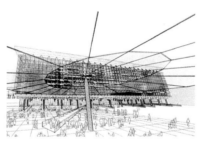

Perspective from plaza underneath parasol.

In the end, and contrary to most expectations, William Alsop won the competition. It seems that the assessors believed Alsop's building to be the most convincing scheme, as well as the most workable practically.

After The Win

After the competition, crucial changes were still to occur. Once the central *Administratif* block had disappeared (which was the result of a protracted period of rationalisation) the resultant single atrium space led to a series of roof 'options', culminating in a fixed ventilated glass covering. The final form of the 'X' columns was resolved, achieving the reduction of the concrete volume involved to a minimum.

The *Deliberatif* had its own distinct evolution, but the actual transformation was sudden. Previously the shell here was an asymmetrical convex cylinder. This defied panel standardisation. Now the shell itself had to become weather-proof, with the removal of the outer 'carapace' on economic grounds. Arups finally conceived the shell as a folded hexagon, made up of a requisite number of identical flat metal panels. The shell was now to cover only half the *Deliberatif*; the remainder allowing the two main internal floors to slice through a glazed wall and to project outwards forming massive balconies – an undoubtedly useful facility given the large numbers likely to use the building. The central core of the *Deliberatif* itself received shelter from the elements by translucent fabric skins, stressed out between the steel spans like sails.

Brian Clarke had ingeniously evolved a method of screen printing a blue design, to suit Alsop's prescription, on the glass of the western façade. The whole issue of colour treatment had been tactically deferred before the final planning approvals. Now a blue model committed all. Clarke's involvement, which had been indicated at the final jury stage, was a wise step. The façade of glass, which changes and deepens in hue throughout the day, was enlivened by a seemingly random patterning of blue. A special depth and variation emerge in this way, relieving the inevitably repetitive scale of the *Administratif* block's exterior. Ultimately, this blue now covers the whole exterior, including the *Deliberatif*. The flanks of the atrium remain a very pale green. This is a marine version of green, the colour of a very shallow,

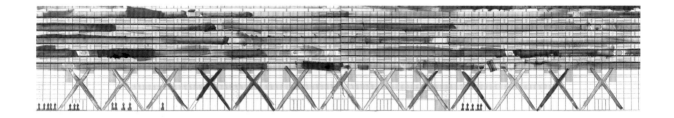

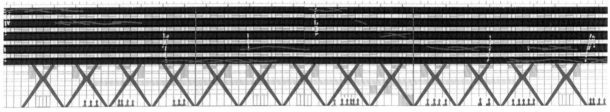

Studies for the façade by Brian Clarke.

sand-swilling bay perhaps, or the outlet of a cave, pale, almost luminescent. However it is the effect of white, transparent glass, produced using white sand initially which is a normal glass production mode.

The scheme to be started on site had survived bureaucracy, local prejudice, numerous changes in mass, profile, and structural solution. The remarkable thing is that it emerged in any way recognisably akin to the original Stage *1* idea. This closeness to the original concept, testifies to its strength.

Post-competition model.

Encore

The Alsop office had, through Jonathan Adams, a competent record; few projects receive such meticulous documentation as this has. This resource has been consulted for a host of detail; Adams has also encapsulated as well as anyone might, and from a deep seam of the whole experience, the nature of this megalith:

> *From its earliest form the building was filled with special spaces, ultimately made more remarkable by the binding of blue. The planning of all parts exploits as far as possible the opportunities of occupying such invigorating forms. The 'Ovoid', itself within a vast space, holds its own space of dreamlike beauty. The conference and debating halls inside the 'Deliberatif', the wonderful external spaces on the*

*balconies of the 'Aerofoil' and the 'Deliberatif', the Block B
roof-terrace and the unprecedented space below the
'Deliberatif' – all these places are hard-won.
Immensely complex, several buildings in one, many
functions, hundreds of rooms, many unique spaces and
experiences: this book barely begins to describe the full
intricacy of the flowering of the first competition diagrams
into the built Hôtel du Département. The building may have
changed since its inception but it is no less new, no less vital,
just as true to Alsop's first intuitive vision, and just as
perfectly real.*

Copains

So the competition was won. The invincible knight was defeated,
and the rank outsider had won. The disappointments of Seville
had been reversed. A tremor shook the architectural world at
large. But the jury's verdict was secure. The press celebrated. At
least here in France there could be no royal intervention, no
'carbuncle' insults to destroy the climacteric. The building that
had won began to seem increasingly plausible. The Marseilles
press was not alienated. The groups of *copains* playing *boules* in
the small park across the way from the site seemed unperturbed
as the site demarcation fences were established. The game went
on.

William Alsop knew that play had only just begun.

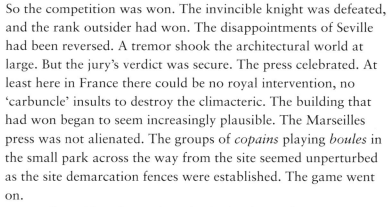

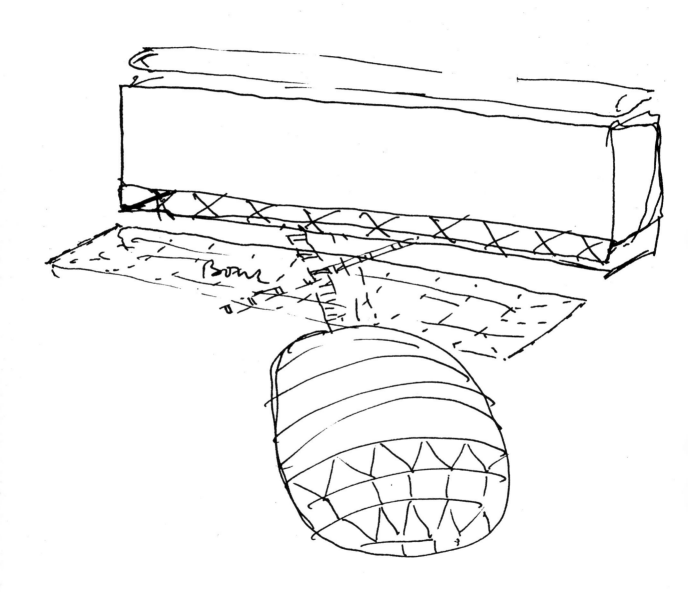

Form Swallows Function*

When the cathedrals were white...

LE GRAND BLEU WAS ONCE WHITE, as we saw earlier. But at the appropriate stage in the competition it emerged as blue from the opaque chrysalis. Yves Klein identified blue ultramarine as a profoundly spiritual blue, and surrounded this element with a mythology that still resonates in southern France, amongst other allusions, of humanity.

Emblematically, the *Hôtel du Département des Bouches-du-Rhône* (HD *13*) now occupies a key peripheral intersection of Marseilles, capital of the region. If you did not know, and had not heard of '*Treize*', you might consider the building to be the headquarters of a leading technology corporation. Certainly it has at least the significance today of, for example, the *Johnson Wax* building (*1936–1939*) by Frank Lloyd Wright. At the initial press viewing of the building in March *1994*, Patrice Goulet, *responsable du Département Création/Diffusion at the Institut Français de l'Architecture* said that the building was 'one of the major realisations of twentieth century France and even Europe, not only in terms of quality and modernism of its architecture, but also for the quality of services and the innovative use of colour in a concrete building'.

Typologically, this is the contemporary counterpart of the historic, highly embellished town or civil halls which abounded throughout Europe as the nineteenth and early twentieth centuries and as witness to the growth of democratic government. The archetypes existed earlier; such great civic architecture was presented by the city halls of Louvain, or Hamburg. More latterly, R. Ostberg's *Stockholm City Hall* (*1906–1923*) re-emphasised the manner in which great cities continued to require architectural distinction to establish their civic eminence.

*With acknowledgments to Paul Finch for the statement.

View from level 7 roof terrace towards block A.

Beaubourg competition entry model.

On deeper comparison of LE GRAND BLEU with such precedent, one comes, however, upon certain anomalies. Of necessity, this site, facing a veritable *place* shared with a major cultural centre for the city of Marseilles, implies an entry to the *Hôtel du Département* on the north–west side of the long elevation of the building as the city's own building dominates the ground level of the place. This effectively detracts from the possibility of an axial approach. Alsop has resolved this shortcoming by re-establishing a new, gently inclined access from the north–west side at ground level, and a new place, at a raised ground floor level. Notwithstanding this, the pedestrian and public entry point remains relatively low-key via sliding doors, at right angles to the main axis of the building, laterally moving past the substantial 'X' columns.

At this point the visitor is immediately aware of the full impact of the atrium space. The sloping floor here convincingly represents 'real' ground level, and a glance to the right at this entry point reveals the distinctive form of the 'Ovoid', placed close to the southern end of the great Atrium *nave*.

View through 'Ovoid' to Atrium.

It is at this point that one is reminded that this is a governmental building, inclusive to a typology that invariably incorporates substantial volumes of bureaucratic office space. LE GRAND BLEU is no exception, and the two parallel and elevated administrative blocks provide such necessities of the *Hôtel du Département* unequivocally. The directional thrust of movement and priority remains lateral to the Atrium however, and Alsop has enhanced this effectively, both by allowing the *Deliberatif* to become distantly visible through the transparent lines of columns in the Atrium, as well as by escalators and bridges between the blocks.

There is no evident historical precedent in the conventional city hall however, as mentioned above. The symbolic differentiation of administration from executive is usually masked within the building envelope. In a period when it is vital that democratic institutions are seen to perform effectively, the relationship of bureaucracy to elected executive authority demands greater visual expression. It is significant to Alsop's win perhaps that the proposal of the runners-up in the final round wholly failed to establish this differentiation, at least externally. The clear 'disarticulation' of such *parti* by Alsop enabled these, and lesser distinctions to become clearly readable, both internally and externally by visitors and passing traffic.

To find a reasonable comparison in the maintenance of such a hierarchy of precedence and function, one must reach farther back in European history, to the Renaissance period. The *Uffizi* building in Florence is famous as a civic art gallery, yet it began life as an overdue regrouping by the Florentine rulers of a loosely dispersed conjunction of city archives and administrative offices. As conceived by Giorgio Vasari and others around *1560*, parallel blocks were inserted at variance to the loose medieval housing grid filling the space between the *Palazzo Vecchio* and the Arno. Entry to these offices was lateral, at right angles to the mannerist directional axis of two-point perspective; Vasari inserted a highly transparent loggia, the 'Loggia dei Lanzi'. This focus (like Alsop's 'Ovoid') was not strictly part of the brief, and

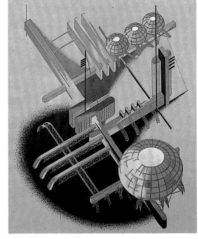

Axonometric representation of refinery. I. Chernikov, *Fantasy* No. 26, 1933

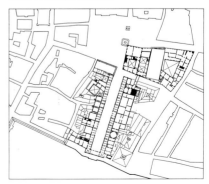

Plan of *Palazzo Uffizi* (1560), with bridge link to *Palazzo Vecchio*.

yet its visual role is critical. It focuses on the Arno beyond (and related routes) and it physically places emphasis on the lateral, first floor bridging role it fulfils. In fact, as with Marseilles, these administrative offices are linked by bridging elements, to each other thereby, and to the seat of government, the *Palazzo Vecchio*. Unlike the *Deliberatif*, this seat of autocratic government (of the Medici family) faces the public square (the 'Piazza della Signoria') and abuts the Uffizi offices to the other end. Here and in visual terms scale and proportion are significant. The separate functions of executive and administration are wholly apparent, in both examples.

Palazzo Uffizi, courtyard.

Such historical parallels need to be approached with caution. However a further source in the confirmation of historical continuity must surely be found in the role of primary structure and the resolution of its connection and correlation within a given scheme's broad grammatical construction. The *Hôtel du Département* demonstrates a highly specific development of columnar supports, in the structural design programme for the two administrative blocks. The unique 'X' columns (whose evolution is described in the Introduction, and Chapter VI) form a transfer structure and permit a doubling of the structural grid from *10.8* metre centres between columns to *5.4* in the administrative blocks.

In Greek classical architecture, the varying entasis of column design as selected created remarkable differences in visual effect. The most robust example of all is not to be found in the centre, Athens, but in the colonial temples created by the Greeks in southern Italy, at Paestum. Here structural power was expressed as it was nowhere else. The columns were the most significant element in the design, in terms of this expression:

> *The columns rise, swell, contract, cushion out into an*
> *upward-thrusting echinus, and stiffen into the slab of the*
> *abacus upon which the weight of the entablature and*
> *pediment is placed. This weight, though solid, no longer*
> *appears to press down upon the columns unduly, nor do*

Atrium view with 'Ovoid'.

Left: Entrance façade block A.

Uffizi linked by bridge to *Palazzo Vecchio*.

Escalator link between block B and the *Deliberatif*.

these any longer dramatise their support of it. The resolution between these forces is so exact as to remove a sense of conflict but not so precise as to preclude variation. Vincent Scully, *The Earth, the Temple and the Gods* (Yale University Press, 1964).

While Scully is referring in this passage to the second temple of Hera (450 BC) the point made is universal. It is precisely this visual and physical balance that Alsop has achieved to perfection, and with remarkable innovation, at Marseilles. Indeed the 'X' columns can be considered an absolute bonus, since they were evolved in the design process well after the competition win. Previous versions displayed vertical columns. While Alsop had considered 'X' columns as early as February *1990*, there had been no resolution that firmly incorporated such a decision until late *1991*.

Final resolution of the primary structural schema allowed a commensurately successful resolution of the support system for the upper level 'Aerofoil' in turn: piloti fit naturally at this level of hierarchy.

The precedent for design solutions is usually sought in previous schemes by the office. The design of the *Deliberatif* incorporates appropriate feedback from previous schemes, notably again that for *EXPO '92* in Seville (as does the form of the 'Aerofoil'). Indeed the 'Ovoid' within the Atrium at Marseilles is a direct importation of the design for the *Cardiff Bay Visitors' Centre*. In its role as a contemporary form of loggia this is wholly legitimate, a practice commonly employed in Renaissance architecture, where significant form is wholly transferable in detail or in entirety.

It is impossible to construct a building of such scale and importance as LE GRAND BLEU in Marseilles without coming to terms with the *unité d'habitation* housing block by Le Corbusier. It is for example significant that the roof terrace of the *unité d'habitation* is surrounded by a chest-level parapet which presents the visitor with the Mediterranean horizon and distant views of the higher ground around Marseilles while excluding wholly the immediate city. Alsop, by contrast, brings the whole and immediate cityscape into spectacular view from on high, and never more so than from the terraces on the administrative block roofs and from the 'Aerofoil'.

View of building in context taken from *Notre Dame de la Garde*.

Such revelations enhance reality rather than abstracting it. LE GRAND BLEU embraces the city of Marseilles. Alsop ensures that occupant and visitor alike to this new citadel can readily orientate with other key landmarks as well as the more immediate surrounding area, as befits a centre of regional government. At every level the elements of the communication system, routes of primary and secondary significance, horizontal and vertical, are clearly differentiated. Alsop has loosened the prescriptive modernist codes of his predecessors, while sustaining the prospect of the new with credibility.

Finally, this concept of political, hence physical accessibility as befits a credible democratic institution of government, is fostered by the colour schemata employed externally and within the Atrium. Literally, LE GRAND BLEU is now codified in its public role by this means. And if only a few people were to notice that the blue chosen is that which is loved by Yves Klein, or that for *Treize*'s centre of government each administrative block has but two rows of thirteen 'X' columns each, it would not matter, least of all to Alsop: for both are pure coincidence. Considerably greater numbers of the populace will respond intuitively themselves to its warmth and symbolism under the sky of the *Midi*, or under the stars at night.

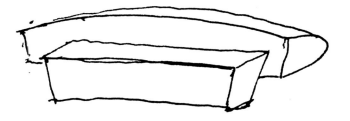

Architect's Note

I WAS FORTY-TWO YEARS OLD WHEN I won the competition for
the *Hôtel du Département* and as I sit in this bar in Vienna I
discover that I am forty-six (yesterday was my birthday). This
project has occupied nearly four years of my life. I used to
expound upon the virtues of designing a building a day. I
explained that the average architect, if he were lucky, might
design fifty buildings in his working life and that the progress
made in that period of say thirty to forty years would be limited.
Architecture is not known for its speed and if we learn from
'doing' we will not learn all we are capable of. I speculated that
a building a day over the same period would produce a greater
understanding of what is relevant, and indeed, not relevant.
Why?

I could have designed *1,460* buildings in the time it has
taken me to work on the *Hôtel du Département*, and in some
ways I have. The reason is to take oneself beyond reason. Logic,
strategy and rationalism are easy. What is much more difficult is
going beyond what one knows in order to allow for exploration,

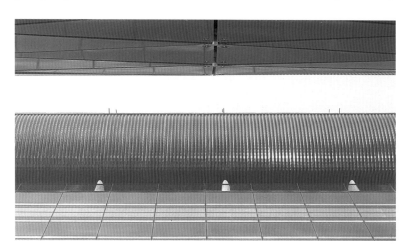

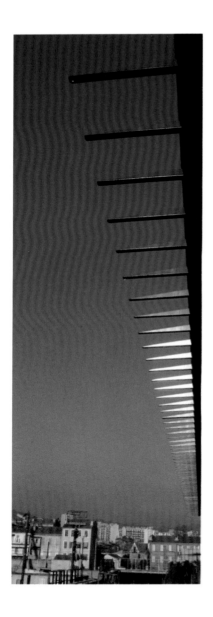

and then to apply the moderating effects of reason. In this way, architecture is discovered and not preconceived.

The *Hôtel du Département* once it was discovered, proceeded to evolve. This process of compromise comes from making the design more public. I usually start work in my studio at the end of my garden by the sea in Sheringham. It commences with sketches, paintings and models. Usually everything is very abstract and slowly ideas, thoughts and aspects of recognition begin to form. Time is also spent looking out of the window, making coffee and drinking whisky. This is not working! Not working is an important part of working. Slowly attitudes arise, often as if from nowhere. I remember the first sketch; it came from Bob Dylan's song 'Shooting Star', thoughts of my half sister Babs who had just died and the planetary nature of some symbol for the *Hôtel du Département*.

This unlikely combination of starting points provided the basis for thoughts on democracy, time and significance. I recall feeling that the building should be open. Here is an edifice paid for by the public purse and occupied by people elected by 'some' of the people who financed it. Usually buildings for both local and central government are unapproachable. They are designed to intimidate. They are designed to instil a feeling of superiority in the people who occupy them. These places harbour first power and then corruption. MY BUILDING SHOULD NOT STIMULATE THIS ETHOS. Inherent in this sketch is also the idea of time. Decentralised power in France is a recent development and I see no reason why it should not change again in the future. Our politics and ideas about administration reflect the values of society which in turn evolves. Who knows the yeffects of a united Europe, for example, on Bouches-du-Rhône? How does one respond to these thoughts with architecture? The building with its expansive floor of arrival was conceived as a large enclosed public square which will complement the external square in front of the building. The building is open. It should be possible to relax in this area with both coffee and a newspaper. Accessibility to this space gives ownership to the people who paid for it, and introduces a sense of 'normal' life into this citadel of administration.

Time is the great unknown. This building in the future can fall into different use. There is no certainty about either the future of the *Département* or indeed the manner in which administration will work. Whether or not the building maintains its existing function, I felt it important that the *Deliberatif*, which contains the spaces of debate, should be conceived as a permanent, inflexible structure. This edifice should always remain a reminder of both good, and bad, decisions made by politicians. The remainder of the building, the *Administratif*, is flexible. It could be easily converted into a hospital, housing or be demolished. I see the life of the centralised office building as one that is limited.

Significance is a quality which changes. The choice of the site, in the northern part of Marseilles, already shows a shift in thinking, from what one supposes a choice of site in *1890* might have been. The latter would have taken a central position that would impose its own importance on the city because of it. Today the choice is bounded on two sides by urban highways in the middle of a run-down quarter. The placement of this building in this location represents the idea of the building as a catalyst: a financial investment that would breathe new life into a depressed area, which might spark further investment in the future. The other possible way of viewing the choice of site is that it represents a 'modern' view of the city. Location is based on accessibility by road, and in this case, *métro*. These remote 'edge' sites spread the city. They represent islands of activity. The logical conclusion of this development is that the *Département* becomes the city and the city becomes a smaller part of the *Département*. POLITICAL ADMINISTRATION MUST CHANGE WITH SOCIAL MOBILITY. The significance of the building in this context had to be considered. The place had no specific meaning. It does not reside in the centre of a town, or even in splendid rural isolation. In the absence of context, the idea of signifying the building had to be approached in another

way. The building should signify itself by its presence. For this reason I employed two devices. The first was to use the 'golden section' to determine the proportion of the building. I have discovered that this classic method gives simple forms a weight which achieves both poise and beauty. The second is the colour. The role of colour in the building is fundamental to the idea of 'presence'. Certain colours have the capacity to suck light into them. I have often witnessed the example of the copper beech tree which achieves this effect. It manages to absorb light which gives it a quiet authority. Klein International and ultramarine blue also have the same quality. Blue was chosen for the *Hôtel du Département* because of the relationship it has with the Mediterranean sky. The success of this matt blue lies in its quietness. It signifies a peaceful ambience to a building that will often contain frenetic behaviour.

I enjoy the building now I know what it is.

William Alsop
Vienna, *13* December *1993*

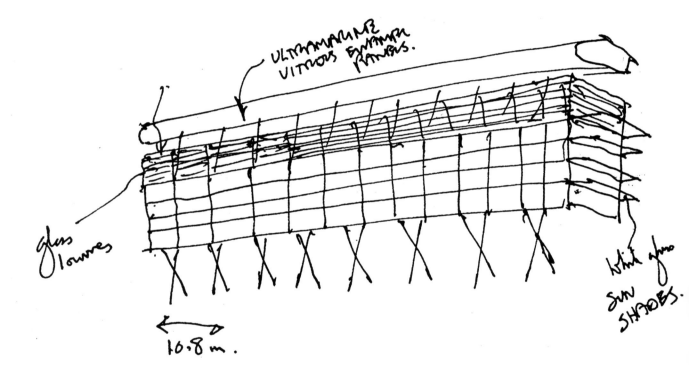

ULTRAMARINE
VITROUS ENAMEL
PANELS.

glass
louvres

White glass
SUN
SHADES.

10·8 m.

Realisation

Contracts and Project Administration

THE CONTRACT WAS SIGNED ON *14* August *1990* between the *Conseil Général des Bouches-du-Rhône* and the winning design team, William Alsop (Architects), Ove Arup & Partners International (Engineers), and Hanscomb Limited (Quantity Surveyors). This was a design team contract from conception to tender analysis.

The President Lucien Weygand with the Director General, *Monsieur* Alain Bartoli, assisted by *Madame* Béatrix Billes, led a client team managed by the *Conseil Général*'s department of Building and Architecture headed by Architect Director Pierre Garnier.

Design development meetings were held in Marseilles and London as scheme design proposals were prepared for the first

Stage I painting.

formal post-competition stage submission in December *1990*. There followed a period of flux as the proposals and the brief were re-analysed and the client team was restructured to include SCIC-AMO/G3A in Paris as project manager and delegated client. This led to a revised brief and a second scheme design submission in April *1991*. The focus of design development and brief analysis then shifted to Paris as the complex technical proposals were developed by the design team and presented to and discussed with SCIC-AMO/G3A and their appointed technical consultants.

Concurrently, the scope of the design team contract was increased to cover site operations and the *Bureau d'Etude* OTH

Combined structural and services plan, as produced by *Cellule de Synthése*.

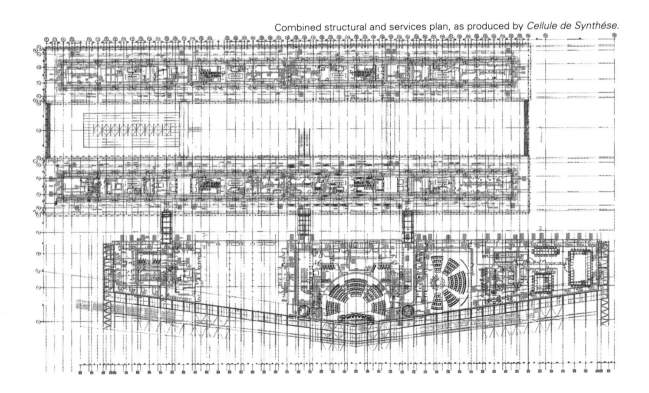

MEDITERRANÉE incorporated into the design and site supervision teams. Detailed design proposals were formally submitted in August *1991* and a planning application of the final scheme was submitted in September *1991*.

In May *1992* an agreement was reached regarding the necessity for an interior design contract. French interior designers were appointed to work with William Alsop on specific areas of the building. Andrée Putman (ECART Paris) was chosen to work on the main spaces in the *Deliberatif* and Charles Bové (Roure-Bové Marseilles) for the mezzanine restaurant and the Elected Members Club.

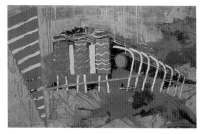

Stage II painting.

The whole project is split into *38* tender packages and tender documentation, prepared in accordance with a programme by GEMO, Project Programmer, employed by the client to ensure a start on site in December *1991* for completion early in *1994*. The issue of tender packages was spread over a period from October *1991* (earthworks package) to December *1993* (signage package).

The complex nature of the building construction, the fast-track programme and the co-ordination of architectural, structural and mechanical tender information with the contractors' workshop drawings, necessitated the setting up of a computer aided design team on site (*Cellule de Synthèse*). All general arrangement drawings were thus co-ordinated and re-checked on site prior to their final issue to the contractors for construction.

Stage III painting.

The *Conseil Général*, SCIC-AMO/G3A, Alsop, OTH, GEMO, all had permanent representatives on site, as did all of the contractors; Alsop taking overall design control, and OTH the technical and financial control assisted by Hanscomb. Contract administration was shared between the design team (OTH/Alsop/Hanscomb), the Project Manager (SCIC-AMO/G3A) and the programmer (GEMO).

Francis Graves

The Site

THE BUILDING IS LOCATED TO the north–west of the *Vieux Port*, the ancient and cultural centre of Marseilles, some ten minutes away by *métro*. The quarter known as *Saint-Just* is mostly residential with some commercial and light industrial activity.

The site, previously tram sheds, waste land and a temporary car park servicing the *métro* station, is bounded to the south and east by dual carriage-ways, two of the main arterial routes feeding downtown Marseilles. To the north and west by an *ad hoc* mixture of high and low residential developments which sandwich a concert hall (a feature development and part of the town of Marseilles' urban regeneration programme) against the main façade of the *Hôtel du Département*.

The disposition of building elements which comprise the *Hôtel du Département* reflects and counterpoises the peripheral infrastructures, responding in turn to climatic conditions, urban environment, transport interchange and pedestrian and vehicular access. The response in design terms to site and brief can be understood by evaluating how the building elements have been sited and pieced together.

The Alsop lexicon is immediately intelligible: the *Deliberatif* almost acting as a phalanx to the adjacent highways protecting the building's administrative centre from the heat, dust, noise and pollution created by the adjacent traffic, whilst the lower of the two administrative blocks, block A, fronts and reflects the quiet rhythm of the public square and concert hall.

The building having survived an arduous design process almost intact, was subjected to minor site modifications made over the two year construction programme in agreement between the design architect, client, and contractor.

As built, the *Hôtel du Département* comprises two basement levels which extend across the site to the peripheral

View of north end of building taken from the east.

Concert Hall

Public Square

Urban infrastructure

Left: 'Ovoid' steel frame under construction.

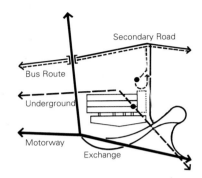

Transport interchange

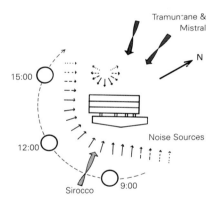

Climate

access roads, connecting together the upper elements of the building, providing car parking, plant rooms, kitchen, various technical facilities and *métro* access. The basement level is where the building straddles the *métro*. As an operational requirement the railway line was kept running throughout the construction programme; the station closed only for two months during the period of construction of transfer beams.

The *Administratif*, located to the south–west, houses the administrative departments of the *Conseil General des Bouches-du-Rhône*. Departments such as community services, financial control, design and architecture are located on the standardised office floors with library facilities, disabled services, restaurant and *crèche* facilities located at ground floor and mezzanine levels. The two blocks A and B are connected together by a semi-climatised atrium.

The Atrium is open to the public and is seen as an extension to the external public square, a political ambition for the project since the competition is epitomised in '*ouvert à tous*', an expression frequently used by the Bouches-du-Rhône President, Lucien Weygand, when explaining the project. Both spaces are of equivalent dimension, the external square gathering together pedestrian access points from the *métro* below the building, and from the bus stops adjacent to the building, moving users towards the main entrance and Atrium via staircases and ramps.

Access to all areas of the building is via the Atrium. Vertical circulation passes through the administration building, via the four lift banks, serving the four storeys of block A and the nine storeys of block B. Access to the *Deliberatif* is across the ground floor slab which slopes at 4 per cent. The idea is a symbolic continuation of the processional route through the centre of the building, via entrance ramps and stairs, taking in the slope across the Atrium floor to reach the base of the escalators. These transport the user through two floors to reach the main entrance halls of the *Deliberatif*. The principal salons (*Séance Publique, Salle Pléniere and the Salon d'Honneur*) lie on an axis with the building's main entrance at ground floor level.

The administration building at all standard levels contains cellular offices arranged around a 'race track' corridor with all service functions, i.e. lifts, staircores, toilets, located within a continuous linear spine.

The *Deliberatif* is physically separated from blocks A and B and can only be reached via the basement levels or by escalator and enclosed bridges located on the upper levels. The bridges between block B and the *Deliberatif* are not only circulation links but ties between two different building forms, the simple block geometry of the *Administratif* and the complex double curved hull of the *Deliberatif*.

The 'Aerofoil', levels 8 and 9, houses the presidential offices, affording the best views of the port and islands beyond. It is separated from the mass of block B on a series of piloti. A linear terrace faces south-west at level 9.

Detail of model showing the 'Ovoid' in the Atrium.

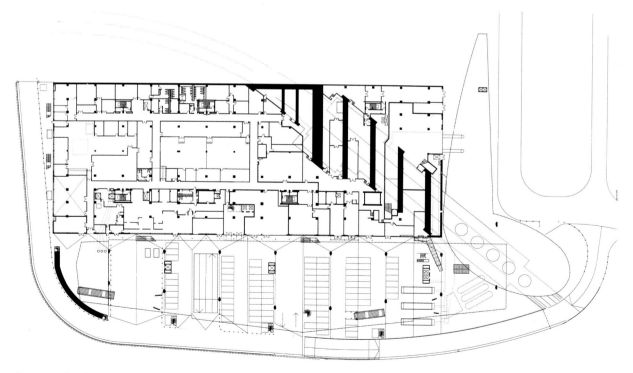

Basement level 1 showing transfer structure over the *métro*.

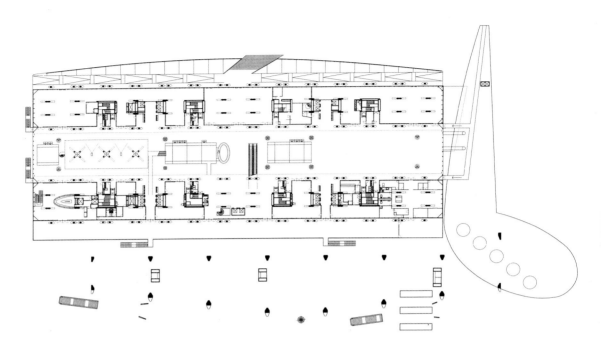

Ground floor plan

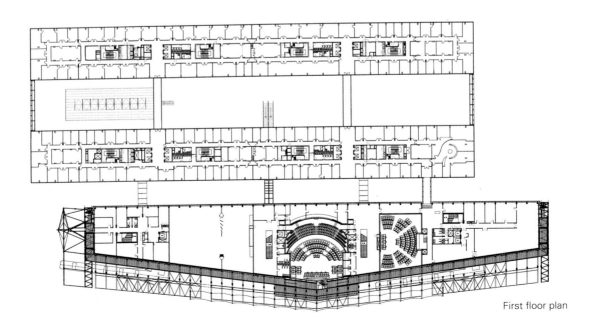

First floor plan

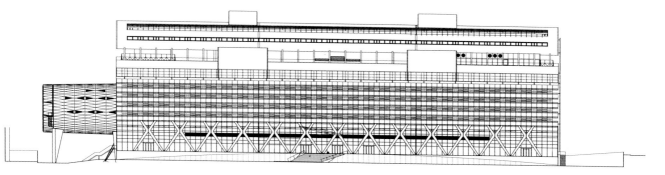

Main façade elevation

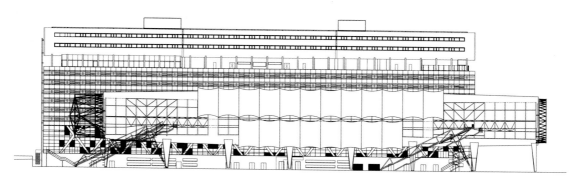

South–east side elevation

Transfer beams over *métro* under construction.

Substructure

The basement levels of the *Hôtel du Département* were constructed using a combination of piled foundations, retaining and diaphragm walls, each dealing in turn with the bespoke geotechnical and physical aspects of the site. The northern end of the *Administratif* sits over the *métro*, necessitating the use of a transfer structure. This carries the load of the *Administratif* on a series of beams which span obliquely across the railway tracks. A system of pre-cast and *in situ* slabs span between the beams to complete the ground floor slab.

The transfer beams were cast *in situ* using specially fabricated steel shutters temporarily supported over the *métro* by a box girder. The beams were cast 50 centimetres above their final resting place, post tensioned in increments and lowered onto their support pads.

The system of construction for the typical basement levels was relatively simple. *In situ* square columns on a 10.80 metre grid support pre-cast beams, in turn supporting concrete floor planks; the rectangular grid so formed is tied together by means of a 15 centimetre thick reinforced concrete topping.

View from basement level 1 towards superstructure of block B.

Superstructure

Administratif

The *10.80* metre structural grid employed for the basement levels is carried through to the ground floor slab using the same method of construction, except at the northern end of the site where it bears onto the transfer structure over the *métro*.

The ground floor slab supports the principal access routes into and around the building. It is at its lowest level on the western boundary: the slab, horizontal below block A and the main entrance, steadily rises across the Atrium at a slope of 4 per cent. It returns to the horizontal below block B and again to a 4 per cent slope for the terrace to the rear of block B.

The *Administratif* structures are formed in concrete using a combination of pre-cast and *in situ* columns and beams, all upper level floors being cast *in situ* on mobile shuttering tables.

The structures are stabilised against asymmetrical wind loading by a combination of *in situ* concrete shear cores surrounding the escape stairs, and upstand beams connecting the perimeter structure with the central cores. The *in situ* stair core

Administratif frame under construction.

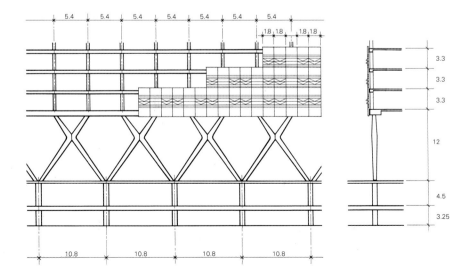

Administratif structural diagram: Two parallel series of 13 'X' columns transfer the established 10.8 metre substructure grid to the 5.40 metre structural grid.

walls are of *25* and *30* centimetre thickness with fins at the lower levels in block B to increase their strength.

Four cores arranged in a linear manner form the central spines of both *Administratif* blocks, providing secondary vertical circulation between basement and roof terrace, while also housing a mixture of service functions: lift batteries, toilets, duct risers and meeting rooms. The lifts are framed with upstand beams to provide fire stops beneath the false floor and for fixing the lift guide rails. These beams also support the blockwork lift shaft walls. Longitudinal and thermal shrinkage along the core and floor plates is controlled by breaking each block into three, with transverse expansion joints at *50* metre centres running behind the stair cores.

The span between the stair cores at typical floor levels is broken by a series of rectangular columns on the *5.40* metre superstructure grid; this, at mezzanine level, transfers back to the *10.8* metre substructure grid via 'V' columns.

'X' and 'V' columns under construction.

'V' and 'X' Column Fabrication

Design engineering decisions taken early during site phase determined the nature of fabrication for the 'V' and 'X' columns. These decisions related to the merits of pre-casting over *in situ* casting and vice-versa. Assessment criteria included: weight and handling difficulties, transport and craning problems associated with off site pre-cast elements and temporary stability on site.

The 'V' columns were for the greater part prefabricated. The two branches of the 'V' were cast in resin-faced plywood shutters, hand finished and delivered to site, they were then temporarily supported on specially fabricated frames. The knuckle-joint between the two branches was then cast *in situ* using a fabricated steel shutter.

The *12.0* metre tall 'X' columns have a spread dimension of *10.80* metres to *5.40* metres, and were cast wholly *in situ*, using steel shutters in four pieces. They were delivered to site from northern France in 'Meccano' kit form, assembled and located in position.

'X' column steel shutter under fabrication at factory in Charleville-Méziere.

The 'X' columns were cast as a single element with on site assembled reinforcement cages using the specially fabricated jigs. The complete cages on stabilising frames were lifted into one half of the 'X' shutters, the frames removed and the shutter closed. The concrete pour was phased to avoid compaction, settlement and vibration problems, using in total three pour points located at equal intervals on the steel shutters. The process from cage construction to finished column took approximately two days.

The *5.40* metre superstructure grid transfers back to the *10.80* metre substructure grid at the *Administratif* gable ends. The typical upper floor plates cantilever outside the line of the 'X' and 'V' columns.

The superstructures were phased in construction from south to north by sequentially rolling and lifting shutter systems. The 'House of Cards' principle was equally employed throughout separate building packages.

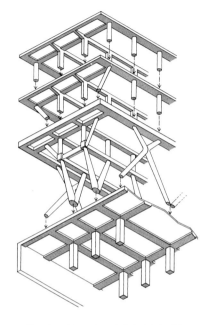

Structural transfer at *Administratif* gable ends.

Next page: First 'X' column being released from its steel shutter.

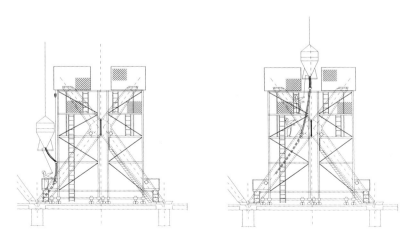

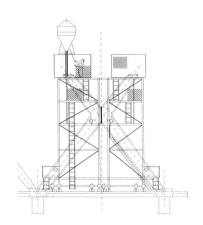

Process of casting the 'X' columns as drawn by the *gros oeuvre* contractor, MCB.

Deliberatif

The overall length of the *Deliberatif* is as the *Administratif*
blocks, *150* metres. On plan the building tapers from *36* metres
at its centre point to *27* metres at both ends, and in section
varies from *20* metres at the centre to *18* metres at both ends.

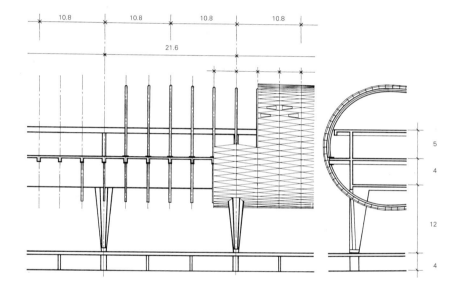

Deliberatif structural diagram:
The structural grid doubles from
10.80 metres to 21.60 metres. This
increase relates to the interface
between the concrete frame and
the steel frame and triangular
cladding panels.

The *Deliberatif* is supported on a series of concrete portal
frames. The frames (legs) bear directly onto columns at
basement level 2, except where a bespoke leg breaks the
structural narrative and lurches away over the *métro* running
below. This deviation visible from the north-eastern corner of
the site characterises the Alsop product code; here, the locals do
not need to approximate the building's subtleties, as a gesture it
leaves an unalterable effect on the individual; a display of
emotion, a sweep of the paint brush which adds to its character.

The *Deliberatif* portal frames were cast in steel shutters. The
leg profile remained the same, the dimensional variation being
taken out in the portal spine. The portals are connected laterally
by floor-high beams.

First *Deliberatif* concrete portal frame
under construction.

Steel ring connection to concrete frame.

The *Deliberatif* superstructure was constructed without movement joints. Movement attributed to shrinkage was negated by phasing the construction from the north and south to the building's centre, allowing settlement and shrinkage to take place prior to the two building halves being tied together.

The structure of the *Deliberatif* can be divided into four elements: the floors, the portal frames, the steel shell enclosure, and the steel balconies.

Frames and Forms

The concrete frames of the 'Aerofoil' and the *Deliberatif* are enclosed using complex and delicately calibrated structural and cladding systems. The design solutions employed for these two parts of the building use a series of transverse steel rings fixed to nodal points on the concrete frames. The skeletal structures were then 'fleshed out' using sheet and panel cladding systems appropriate to the building form.

The *Deliberatif* frame is made up of 244 millimetre diameter tubular steel rings on a 3.60 metre linear grid, transportation, storage, erection and complexity of site welding determined that each ring was fabricated in three sections. At level 1, vertical support to each ring is provided by posts in front of the glazing line. To the east the ring is supported horizontally and vertically by a cantilever truss. The nodal point where the vertical post and truss meet is where the ring is fixed to the concrete rib structure, the bottom chord of the truss also provides support to the 'clip-on' balcony structures. The second part of the ring forms the *Deliberatif* enclosure, connecting at high level to the cantilever truss behind the glazing line, and at its base via a steel shoe to the slab edge of level 2. The final component is the part of the ring below the level 1 slab. This is a simple beam supported at points off the concrete and radiused to form the *Deliberatif*'s underbelly.

Relative movement between the steel and concrete structures is minimal, given that the majority of the steel frame is

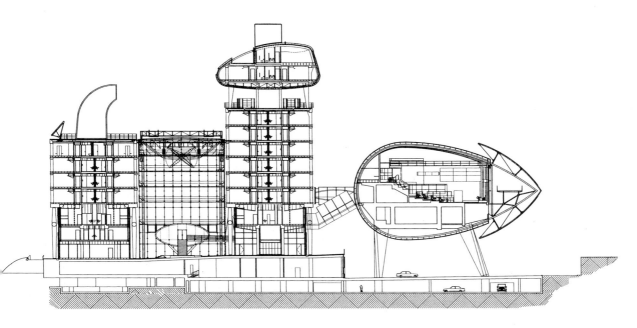

Cross-section

internalised and protected from significant temperatures changes by the building cladding system.

Lateral stability to the steel frame is provided by portal action and in its longitudinal direction by horizontal trusses between the rings. The steel structure does not rely on the panel cladding system for longitudinal stiffness. The portion of the steel frame external to the building envelope is subject to movement and is isolated at the building's centre. Here longitudinal restraint is omitted, allowing the building's two extremities to move independently.

On paper, the form of the *Deliberatif* has a simplistic symmetry; however, faced with the prospect of executing first the steel frame and then the cladding, it was soon realised how complicated this process would prove. Following closely the outline fabrication and construction proposal contained within the tender documentation, an in-depth analysis by the consultant and contractor teams was carried out. Conclusions for both the fabrication and constructional logistics were as follows:

All component elements of the steel frame were prefabricated, the three constituent elements of each ring were

Deliberatif tambour structure being craned into position.

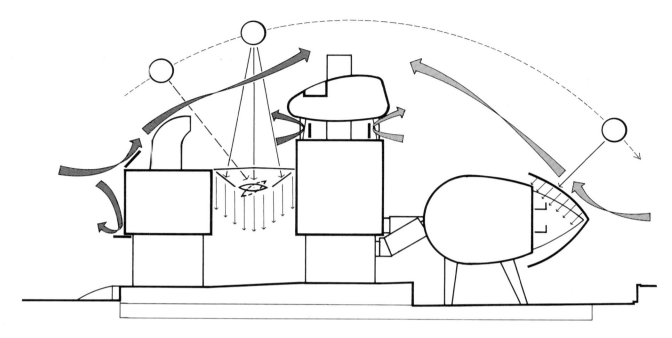

Response of building form to specific environmental criteria: The above transverse section indicates how the building is protected from severe east–west solar and wind conditions.

The geometry of each of the steel rings is defined by three circles, the diameter of which varies along the building's length; the larger rings in the centre decrease towards the north and south, forming the distinctive double-curved wing shape.

rolled, pre-cambered and kit assembled in the factory; laid to a drawn template to ensure fabrication accuracy prior to site delivery. The ring components were erected in sequence commencing with the largest 'nose' section. This was lowered onto the studs cast into the concrete ribs and temporarily fixed and supported while the second element which forms the building enclose was craned into place, supported, fixed at its base and welded to the nose section. The rings were installed in batches of three, giving the growing frame lateral stability. The third element, forming the underbelly, was fixed at a much later date having no programmatic implications on the building's water tightness.

The *Deliberatif* form created by the varying dimension steel rings is a complex three-dimensional shape made up from eccentric conical surfaces. Viewed as a folded out plan the wing is made up out of standardised triangular panels fixed between the steel rings on a 3.60 metre grid. Here the cladding system

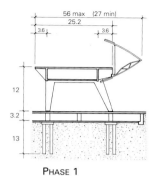

56 max   (27 min)
25.2
3.6   3.6
12
3.2
13

PHASE 1
Front edge and Truss

PHASE 2
Back Bone

Primary insulated
chassis frames fixed
to steel rings.

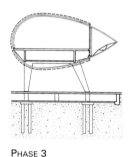

PHASE 3
Underbelly and Skin

PHASE 4
Sun screen/Wind
deflector and Bridges

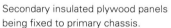

Secondary insulated plywood panels
being fixed to primary chassis.

can be viewed in its pure rhythmic state. However, when folded over the skeletal steel structure, the simplistic geometry becomes over-constrained, and must distort to take the form required.

The principle of the triangular panel geometry, as developed for the *Deliberatif*, is consistent throughout a typical cross-section of the building skin.

The imperfection of the triangular panel geometry is modified in the joints between adjacent panels; each joint being irregular allowing the necessary degree of geometrical distortion.

The component parts of the *Deliberatif* skin were pre-fabricated, site-assembled and phase-fixed sequentially with the *Deliberatif* steel ring structure. First, triangular galvanised steel chassis frames with rigid insulation panels were mechanically fixed to stainless steel 'stems' which had been pre-bolted to the steel rings. Each stem provided the fixing points for six chassis

External triangular aluminium skin, fixing plates and waterproof membrane.

frames, reducing significantly the number of eventual penetration points through the building's waterproof membrane. Second, triangular plywood decking panels were screwed via cavity spacers to the chassis frames below, the cavity created between the two layers providing internal ventilation. The varying dimension slots between the decking panels giving the external skin its elasticity and ability to achieve the required double curvature, were packed with compressible insulation. Third, the waterproof membrane was strip-laid over the plywood decking panels and the overlapped joints welded together; special waterproof sleeves were used to provide a clean joint between the fixing stems and membrane penetration points. Fourth, triangular aluminium powder coated cassettes, with an internal anti-drumming compound, were bolted to the part of the stem fixing visible above the plywood decking panels.

The internal skin of the *Deliberatif* follows the same pattern as the external skin. Here two sheets of *13* millimetre plasterboard cut into triangles are fixed to the inside face of the steel chassis. The base plasterboard panels are covered in some areas with cushioned fabrics appropriate to location and acoustic requirements.

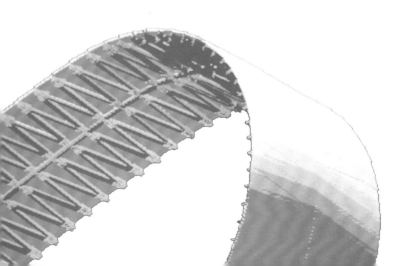

Computer generated model of *Deliberatif* skin.

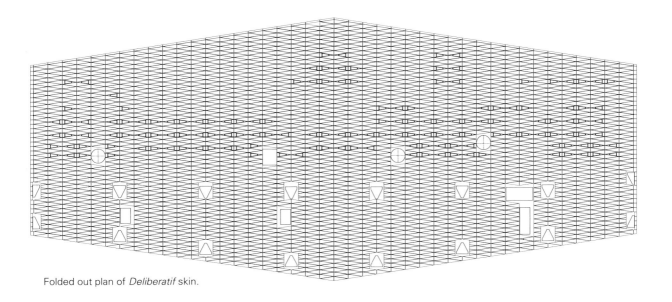

Folded out plan of *Deliberatif* skin.

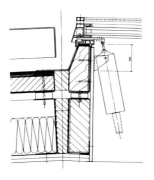

Typical cross-section through *Deliberatif* skin.

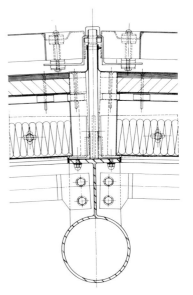

Completed *Deliberatif* skin.

Block B level 7 terrace, below the
'Aerofoil'.

Aerofoil

The 'Aerofoil' steel frame, as that of the *Deliberatif*, connects at prescribed points back to the concrete superstructure. The frame consists of a series of transverse ribs at *5.40* metre centres, which were fabricated in five sections. The lower three elements are short tee sections rolled to form the external faces of level eight and the underbelly of the 'Aerofoil'. The sections were post fixed to the underside of edge beams at levels *8* and *9* and hung at central points from the level nine slab. The two primary upper elements of the 'Aerofoil' frame are fabricated steel tee beams bolted to either side of a single off-centre cantilevered column and to the edge beams of level *9*.

The 'Aerofoil' is finished internally with two skins of *13* millimetre plasterboard laid with staggered joints and screwed to the trapezoidal internal metal deck. Negative joints are located against the flange of the fabricated tee section which is exposed.

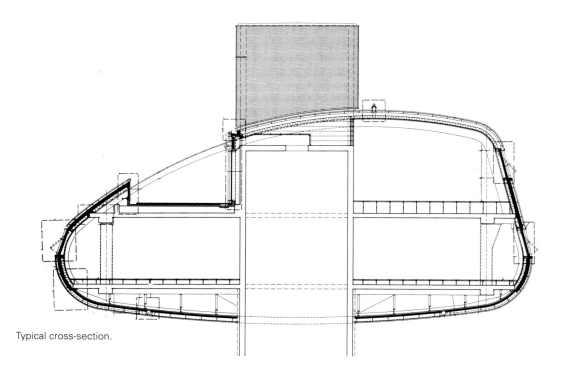

Typical cross-section.

'Ovoid' under construction, sited at the south end of the Atrium.

Previous page: View of 'Aerofoil' looking south across the Atrium roof.

Ovoid

The 'Ovoid' is a multifunctional pod sitting at the south end of the Atrium. Similarly to the *Deliberatif* and the 'Aerofoil' it has a primary concrete frame with a 'clip-on' steel structure. The concrete floor slab structure is supported on precast quadropartite 'V' columns spanning in both longitudinal and transverse directions. The slab was formed *in situ*, spanning between edge beams that connect and tie together the heads of the 'V' columns. Structural stability is provided by frame action longitudinally with a moment connection at the base of the 'V' columns in a transverse direction.

The steel framework consists of a series of transverse ribs at 2.70 metre centres rolled to form the ovoid shape. The ribs were fabricated from steel plate to form the sections. They are tied longitudinally together at 1.8 metre centres with the end two bays being cross braced within the depth of the rib structure to stop racking. Lateral stability to the steel frame is provided by portal action and longitudinal stability by a combination of portal action from the transverse spanning 'V' columns and girder action from the inclined crossbracing.

The cladding is nonstructural. The 'Ovoid' acts as an acoustic baffle to the Atrium. Behind the perforated cladding 5 centimetres of medium density wool insulation is packed between the internal plasterboard skin and steel ribs. Each ring supports two motorised wings fixed at mid points; the wings support opaque panels facilitating slide projection and exhibition space when in a vertical position. Both gable walls of the ovoid are structurally glazed. Linear skylights in single skin, translucent polycarbonate sheet run centrally along its roof.

'Ovoid' steel frame during erection.

Façades

The elements that comprise the *Hôtel du Département* façade package can be separated into three categories. They are:

   i) The *Administratif* primary façades
   ii) The Atrium roof and Atrium gable façades
   iii) Secondary façade systems

Administratif Primary Façades

The typical upper levels of the *Administratif* buildings were clad using standardised prefabricated glazing modules; the panel dimensions being *1.8* metres wide to suite the *5.40* metre superstructure grid and *3.30* metres high so that horizontal panel joints occurred below the transparent fenestration line at mid points on typical floors.

    The panels were craned directly from the delivery lorries to their pre-determined position on the façade, where the

Panels being craned into position.

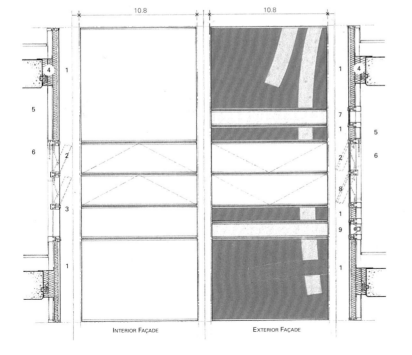

INTERIOR FAÇADE   EXTERIOR FAÇADE

1 Insulated glass panel
2 Opening lights: single glazed
3 Single glazed panel
4 Fire break
5 Opaque aluminum cladding panel
6 Blinds
7 Double glazed translucent panel
8 Opening lights: double glazed
9 Double glazed translucent panel backlit
   with a blue fluorescent tube

External façade.

Internal façade.

installation teams guided the suspended panels from the floor edges to their fixing points. The panels were anchored back to the floor edge beams via cast-in Halfen rails and a male/female hook system. Adjustment and finished tolerance between adjacent panels was achieved using secret mounted levelling screws and vertical expansion joints. Each cladding module comprised a primary steel frame of transoms and mullions with a palette of infill panels appropriate to location and function.

External Façades

A realised ambition for the external façade was that it should absorb Marseilles' special blue daylight quality while remaining totally matt and non reflective. A special glass was developed in conjunction with the facade contractor Structal Rinaldi and St-Gobain, the glass manufacturer. The product of site and factory testing is a 6 millimetre glass with a printed surface of small indentations, which renders the glass surface matt in daylight conditions, meeting the prescribed design criteria. The base blue colour of the façade was chosen over a long protracted process involving the client, architect, artist (Brian Clarke), project manager, contractor and manufacturer. It is true to say that more time was spent discussing the base colour of the building façades than for any other element of the building. The agreed blue, a close approximation to the blue of the painter Yves Klein, was enamelled onto the internal face of the glass at the Aniche factory of St-Gobain. Here Brian Clarke's façade design based on choreographic notation was translated from the full-size design original to photographic templates and then silk screened onto the glass panels. Colour combinations using various shades of blue were prototyped and matched to Brian Clarke's coloured original. The panels were delivered to site and fixed temporarily in position for assessment as Clarke had insisted (in all types of light conditions), prior to the definitive colour combination being chosen.

The blue panels are combined with, at typical floor levels, transparent opening windows and translucent light slots; the lower of which is back-lit using a continuous blue linear light tube, visible at night as turquoise blue bands which circumnavigate the administrative blocks.

Internal Façades

Internally the Atrium façades used the same specification of St-Gobain printed glass; here, however, the glass was enamelled white – the thickness of the glass rendering the visible surface a cool mint green. The transparent glazed modules of the internal façades were single glazed as opposed to the double glazed external façades, assisting with passive heat gain and cooling of the Atrium: the opening windows of the two façades are bottom hung to prevent smoke ingress in fire conditions. Both the internal and external opening windows were fitted with contact switches which automatically cut out the air conditioning and heating units when the windows are deployed.

Atrium Roof and Gable Façades

The Atrium roof is supported on 219 millimetre diameter tubular steel trusses which span the 18 metres between the facades of the administrative blocks A and B. The trusses sit on corbels which cantilever from the level 5 edge beams into the Atrium void. The trusses also provide support for the fixed and motorised sun shading devices and the suspended gable end structural glazing.

Atrium south gable wall under construction.

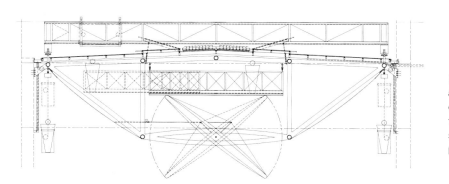

Detail of Atrium gable wall: The baffles are controlled by roof mounted solar censors which relay information back to the BMS enabling the baffles to track the sun's path, preventing direct sunlight penetrating into the Atrium.

The most effective pattern of opening vents relating to latent wind conditions is established automatically by roof mounted wind censors, these relay information back to the Building Management System (BMS) which selects the appropriate pre-programmed series of openings at roof level and air intake balance ventilation at ground floor level.

The roof mounted sun shading comprises two types: first, a raked tensile sun screen is clipped to the underside of the roof trusses and permanently fixed in position, and second, motorised solar baffles (an aluminium wing shaped frame with a tensile sun screen covering) which pivot around the axis of the lower web of the roof trusses.

The north and south structurally glazed gable walls are supported at each floor level by horizontal trusses which span the *18* metre-wide Atrium, assisted by mid point hanging positions from the special gable roof trusses. The trusses also serve as maintenance access gantries. Given that the *Administratif* blocks A and B deflect independently (resulting in differential movement across the gable walls), the system of suspension employed allows the deflection and movement across the plane of the gable wall to occur.

The glazing system was designed to sit flush with the gable walls of the *Administratif* blocks with vertical expansion joints providing adjustment tolerance and two dimensional flexibility. The structural glazing system comprises *19* millimetre laminated, toughened glass with stainless steel flush bolt fixings back to node connection points on the horizontal trusses.

Secondary Façade Systems

The first floor of the *Administratif* is elevated *12.0* metres above the ground floor slab. The building envelope between these levels is set back behind the plane of the 'X' columns, providing a deliberate break point between the two installed glazing systems. This allows the structural silicone glazing of the upper levels (the blue *Administratif* box) to float above the ground floor and suspended mezzanine floors, only anchored to ground

Atrium roof trusses during installation: The roof comprises a standard transom and mullion system with transparent and translucent glazing panels. Either side of the ridge beam the roof incorporates glass smoke and fresh air ventilation louvres, both of which are controlled by the BMS. The system of smoke ventilation developed in conjunction with the University of Bristol who carried out wind and aerodynamic tests, relies for its effective operation on a wind deflector mounted on the roof terrace of block A. The Mistral wind which arrives from the north–west is thus deflected up and over the Atrium roof towards the 'Aerofoil'; this prevents eddy currents developing over the smoke ventilation panels which would force the escaping smoke back into the Atrium.

by the blue 'X' columns. The ground and mezzanine floor glazing is more transparent than the upper levels, allowing cross views from the building's exterior to the Atrium, from the ground floor to the mezzanine restaurant and vice-versa.

The glazing system comprises two parts, a rectangular steel hollow section spanning between the ground and first floor slabs carrying required electrical services, and a thermally broken aluminium extrusion which carries the variety of infill panels: transparent and translucent glazing, opaque and louvred panels. The external elements of the facade are sun screened by external automatically controlled louvre blinds.

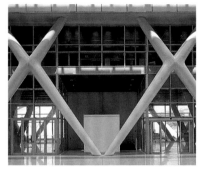

Detail of *Administratif* secondary glazing.

The same glazing system was used for the upper levels of the *Deliberatif*; given however, the lower floor-to-ceiling heights the depth of the aluminium extrusion was sufficient to span unbraced. The glazing was anchored at the slab edge of level 2 which allowed the differential movement between the steel frame and skin to be taken out at the head of the glazing via a sliding connection.

The northern and southern extremities of the *Deliberatif* are sun screened (as the *Administratif*) using external louvre blinds. However the centre section is shaded and protected from the Sirocco wind by a tensile Teflon canopy suspended from a trussed tubular steel structure, which is connected back to the primary steel frame.

Stephen Pimbley

Blue

FROM SPACE THE EARTH IS BLUE: terrestrial blue!

Blue elemental: blue celestial

blue marine

blue aerial

blue aquatic

blue atmospheric

blue diurnal/ blue nocturnal: blue the colour of time:
blue of dawn blue of dusk blue of noon blue of midnight

distant blue/ deep blue: blue the colour of space:
blue of air blue of water blue of sky blue of sea

transparencies of blue! translucencies of blue! – *clarities* of blue!

richnesses of blue: aquamarine/ ultramarine/ lapis lazuli/ cerulean/ azure/ indigo/
sapphire/ electric/ turquoise/ cobalt/ ice

No metaphor no symbol/ but the blue itself.
as: sky blue/ sea blue/ river blue

beauty of blue! simplicity of blue! joy of blue!   magnitude of blue!

Grandeur of Blue

Mel Gooding, May 1994

Finale

WILL ALSOP'S HOTEL DU DÉPARTEMENT for the Bouches-du-Rhône region of France is a building in exile. For a start it is the work of an English architect. Secondly, it is in visual exile – a deep blue intruder into the light Mediterranean browns of the local vernacular.

I could take this point further: for example, this is a highly polished, carefully proportioned building in the midst of a very cluttered, ad hoc landscape. In addition, its forms seem at first glance to be echoed nowhere else in this city. This is, apparently, a rebellion against context, an almost aggressive insistence that *these* forms and *this* colour are right *in spite of* this place.

Yet, in other terms, the building is highly tuned to its context. It is designed to manage and exploit the dry, debilitating winds that sweep this area. It has a slow and a fast side – the first a calm essay in proportion for the pedestrian approach, and the second a more extreme and expressive sculptural form to catch the eye of the driver on the major roads that define two sides of the site.

Furthermore, it is distinctly aware of its political context. This is a centre of government and Alsop had made it directly address, if not its actual constituents, then, at least, the people. The balconies and walkways around the council chamber oblige the politicians to look outwards to the slightly depressed area of the city in which the building is set. Even the highly sculptural feel of the *Deliberatif*, as well as its post-tensioned concrete structure, signal that this is a place where something decisive, something distinctive, something effective is intended to take place. This is a signal as much to the civil servants occupying the building as to the people outside.

I believe this political aspect combined with the strong feeling of intrusion and exile provide important clues to the

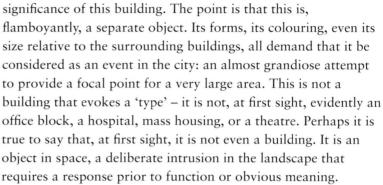

significance of this building. The point is that this is, flamboyantly, a separate object. Its forms, its colouring, even its size relative to the surrounding buildings, all demand that it be considered as an event in the city: an almost grandiose attempt to provide a focal point for a very large area. This is not a building that evokes a 'type' – it is not, at first sight, evidently an office block, a hospital, mass housing, or a theatre. Perhaps it is true to say that, at first sight, it is not even a building. It is an object in space, a deliberate intrusion in the landscape that requires a response prior to function or obvious meaning.

I could clarify this point further through experiment. Imagine Rogers' and Piano's *Pompidou Centre* on the same site. The very first response might be the same: what on earth is that? But, with the *Pompidou Centre*, various possible associations would at once swing into action. It looks industrial, maybe an oil refinery; its overall form is a simple rectangle, so you are clearly required to look into the building for more information. In addition, its vivid celebration of functionality would signal clearly enough that the primary key to this building lay in activity and movement. But no such associations interfere with the first contemplation of Alsop's building. It does not resemble anything else and its forms are generally closed. The very solidity of its blueness both isolates it from the surroundings and starkly delineates its shape. This is obviously, before it is anything else, an object demanding your attention as an object.

This implies a superfluity about the building: it is more than the sum of the usual architectural parts – function, context and so on. It might be said that the same is true of all buildings, even the *Pompidou Centre* evidently exists as an object at a purely aesthetic existence. But the difference here is that this superfluity is not a by-product – something that occurs simply because of the way function and/or context are expressed – but rather it appears to be prior to all such considerations. This is evidently an object-building that can not be justified or determined by any internal rationale. Its sculptural existence is free of explanation and quite intentional.

This gesture obviously amounts to a critique of prescriptive modernism in architecture. In many of its incarnations modernism demanded structural and functional truth, a simplification of forms and a refusal of expressive gesture. In high-tech modernism this became an aggressive, mannered celebration of function. However this effectively revealed the inconsistency of the position – in sculpturally refining the functional elements the high-tech architects were admitting that a degree of poetry had to be returned to the design process unless all buildings were to ossify, with flawless logic, into more or less slick versions of modernist one-liners. By so aggressively detaching the Marseilles building's sculptural identity from its function and context, Alsop is saying: let us no longer kid ourselves, before they are anything else, good buildings are beautiful objects in space.

Of course, running alongside this modernist debate are the anti- and post-modernist debates. These tend to centre on the issue of decoration in that both anti- and post-modernists are impatient with the high moralism of the modernist demand for the removal of all ornament as structurally or functionally 'untrue'. Again the rigour of the modernist position is deceptive – there are many example of supposedly modernist buildings with features that can only plausibly be seen as decoration.

Nevertheless, the easy return of old forms of decoration – Classical, Gothic, whatever – is even less convincing. The reason decoration became a problem was that the old forms and symbols had been emptied of their meaning. They did not quite work any more and so, in the absence of God or victory, function and structure came to be seen as the only meanings that could reasonably be celebrated.

Alsop has indulged in some straightforward decoration at Marseilles – notably in the Brian Clarke murals on the façade. But the real point is that the whole building is decoration. The design superfluity which I referred to earlier is an answer not only to the problems of late modernism but also to the issue of ornament and meaning. Certainly there are problems with

finding a decorative language for our time. But these problems are, if not solved, then at least legitimately avoided if the whole building is turned into a decorative gesture.

This brings me back to the themes of exile and politics with which I began. Evidently the theme of exile relates to Alsop's determination to assert the building's presence as an autonomously beautiful object. It needs to have a line drawn around it, it needs to stand out so that it can be perceived and then judged as a separate, distinctive object. But this beauty is not an entirely remote concept. This is, after all, a centre of government, a place of power and representation. Once such places may have been given authority by columns and porticos. Under a modernist dispensation, that authority may have been denied, supposedly democratically, and government offices and assemblies would come to look much like other buildings. But here authority is restored by asserting the presence of the building as an intense sculptural gesture. We know at first sight that this thing, whatever it is, has significance in this landscape.

In insisting on the aesthetic autonomy of his buildings, Alsop offers the possibility of an architecture free of the rigid ideologies of modernism and its successors. It would be a way of reclaiming the assertive symbolic grandeur of buildings without resorting to the recreation of past styles. This approach leans heavily on the gifts of the architect and might, in lesser hands, lead to catastrophe. But, for the moment, the building that makes this pivotal point in the history of architecture belongs to Marseilles and it is a building that, triumphantly, works.

Bryan Appleyard

The Team

Design Team

William Alsop Architects Architect William Alsop **Directors** Francis Graves Stephen Pimbley **Team** Jonathan Adams James Allen Sonia Andrade Peter Angrave Hilary Bagley Russell Bagley Stephan Biller Florence Bobin Pierre-André Bonnet James Brearley Joanne Burnham Xavier D'Alençon Jason Dickinson Sybil Diot-Lamige Robert Evans Roger Farrow Colin Foster Cristina García Borja Goyarrola Ivan Green Astrid Huwald Stephen James John Kember David Knill-Samuel Nigel Lusty Harvey Male Paul Mathews Roger Minost Philippe Moinard Suzy Murdock Simon North Sophie Palmer Victoria Perry Emmanuelle Poggi Sanya Polescuk Geoffrey Powis John Prevc Mathew Priestman Stuart Rand-Bell Christian Richard Anne Schmilinsky Diana Stiles Peter Strudwick Gary Taylor George Tsoutsos Nicki Van Oosten Laurence York Moore Petra Wesseler **Babel** Michel Seban **Roure Bové** Charles Bové Thierry Ciccione Martine Roure **Ecart S.A.** Andrée Putman Gérard Borgniet Gilles Leborgne Elliot Barnes Marion Guidoni **Hanscomb Ltd.** **Directors** Mike Staples David Wright **Team** Simon Birchall Andrew Blythe Ben Goodenough Stuart Guy Isabelle Lamour-du-Caslou Trevor Powers Mike Stock-Ledwidge **Jolyon Drury Consultancy** **Directors** Jolyon Drury Derek Allcard **Team** Peter Fairchild Geoff King **Casso Gaudin** Jean-Marc Casso Marcel Roland **Ove Arup & Partners International** **Director** John Pilkington **Team** Andrew Allsop David Anderson Pierre Balosso Mike Banfi Guy Battle Sean Billings Alan Burfoot Peter Chapman Phil Connor Colin Darlington Marcial Echenique Colin English Martin Fenn Ghislaine Frayssignes Alistair Hughes Colin Jackson Chris Judd Man Kang Robert Lang Keith Lay Cw Li Alain Marcetteau Joanna Massey Chris McCarthy Hugh Muirhead Maurice Mullaly Dominic Munro Neil Noble Paul Pompili Clodâgh Ryan Manan Shah Ian Smith Mike Summers Jean-Paul Velon Martin Walton Jonathan Ward Terry Watson **University of Bristol, Aerospace Engineering** G. Breeze T.W. Everett T.V. Lawson **Artist** Brian Clarke **GEPAC** Jean-Claude Vogelweid Claude Ginoux Nicole Nourayre **Low Energy Unit** Mike Wilson **OTH Méditerranée** **Directors** Henri Mercier René Leduc Raphaël Saavedra Paul Reginato **Team** Bruno Alligier Jean-Marie Besse Guy Bizet Joseph Campo Jean De Nicola Gérard Desio Véronique Fraysse Jean-Luc Gautier Philippe Kozoulia Jean-Louis Maffeo Gérard Marrot Jean-Pierre Mas Jean Massetto Jean-Paul Matheoud Hélène Miroux Michel Mourot Joelle Pons Jean-Paul Rigail Jean-Jacques Rippert Serge Sanchís Gérard Schoettel Patrick Veyrunes **Cellule de Synthese** Sylvie Corbani Denis David Bruno De Tervis **Averous Bonnel Tarrazi** **Director** Pierre Averous **Team** François Averous Christophe Coquard Serge Dallest Mark Durand-Rival Fabrice Fabiano Philippe Gouirand Sylvie Houbaux Hélène Marmande

Client Team

Conseil Général des Bouches-du-Rhône Président Lucien Weygand **Comité de direction** Alain Bartoli Béatrix Billes **Département des Bâtiments et de l'Architecture** Pierre Garnier Christian Boucherie Alain Delanoye Jean-Marie Estrabaut Robert Malatesta Jean-Claude Martin Jean-Claude Mercadier Jean-Claude Mourey **SCIC-AMO** **Paris** Roger Damiani Hervé Le Huede Fouzi Djazani **Marseille** Georges-Henri Grau Serge Meregalli Bruno Aymard Pascale Abeijon Soraya Ait-Arab Patrick Amico Henri Amigon Jean-Paul Bonnet René Darcy R. Dumas Francette Ernst Véronique Fabri Nasr Fattouche Gérard Hoffmann François Le Clezio Michel Lerasle Bernard Martin Loïc Pingris Joëlle Retailleau Alain Rohat René Sauron **G3A** Gilbert Mouillon René Fournigault Dominique Clavel Claude Mousny Caroline Sagorin

Contractors

Ground works **Entreprise Marion** Deep foundations/Piling **Solétanche** Concrete superstructure/Infrastructure provision **CBC/MCB** Blockwork **CBC/MCB** Steel work/Primary steel cladding **Cabrol** Waterproofing **Spapa** Façades/Roof glazing **Rinaldi Structal** Public health/Fire protection systems **Réservé/SAET/Énergétique & Sanitaire** Electrical installations **Cegelec/EI/SNVD/CIREM** Security installations/Small power installations/Internal communication provisions **Cegelec/EI/SNVD/CIREM** Building management system **GMAO/EI** Telephone installations **Matra Communication Méditerranée** Security systems **Verger Deleporte** Document handler **Fluidelec** Mechanical installations (heating/ventilation) **Albouy/AIC/TNEE** Lifts/Escalators **Otis** Kitchen fit out **Sermofroid/AFP** Metalwork **SPT SA** Raised flooring **Denco** Internal Joinery **Delta Menuiseries** Demountable partitions **Clestra Hauserman** Fixed furniture **Bareau** Hard finishes **Gambini** Soft finishes **Jolisol** Painting/Mirrors **Cantareil** Signage **Lettre & Lumière** Suspended ceilings **Wanner Isofi** Desk lighting **Concord** SLI External works/Landscaping **Sogev** Audiovisual **Entreprise Industrielle/Atelier Sud Vidéo** Secondary steel structures **Cabrol** Dry partitions **Séquence 3/SME/SEGCM/Mercurio**